ask
melissa myers

♡ Jenn
You're Photo-Rogue!
keep taking
great pics &
videos :)

Warmly,
melissa

5-3-22

2-3-99

Mom,

You said,
"You can do whatever it is you set your mind to."
Thank you.
I dedicate this book to you!

Melissa

melissa myers

financial planner

You're wise. You know you need to plan ahead. If you'd like help getting your values and money in alignment so that you can live your ideal life and be a blessing to others,

I can help you!

Curious about learning more?

Phone or Zoom. Schedule a FREE 15-minute call:
https://go.oncehub.com/MelissaMyers

Download your
FREE BONUS
Passport to
Freedom Workbook

passport.askmelissamyers.com

Publishing and Design:

EPIC AUTHOR
PUBLISHING

Ordering Information: Special discounts are available on quantity purchases.

Contact: melissa@askmelissamyers.com | www.AskMelissaMyers.com

First Edition

Going

ROGUE!

UNCONVENTIONAL *FINANCIAL STRATEGIES* FOR *WOMEN*

MELISSA MYERS, CFP®

What People are Saying about *Going* ROGUE!

"Value-driven financial planning shouldn't be a new concept, but Melissa makes it feel revolutionary. She removes the intimidation and emotion from our relationship with money and replaces it with logical and applicable strategies for creating wealth. These strategies are effective for anyone. However, this book specifically speaks to women's unique relationship with money and empowers us to structure our finances to allow us to follow our dreams."

—**Sarah Kallio**, co-author of *The Stocked Kitchen*

. . .

"Relatable and relevant."

—**Carly Niemier**, Human Resources Director

. . .

"If you know where you want to go in life, you can develop a plan for your money. Melissa lays out a financial game plan that is so simple and easy to follow. I wish I would have known some of these insights earlier, but I'm glad I found this book when I did. It's never too late. Don't wait."

—**Tammy Stone**, realtor, Key Realty

. . .

"Melissa walks her talk. She doesn't preach. She lives it. I thought my life was well-balanced. Looking back, I see that it wasn't. Now that I have balance and my priorities in order, I can justify lifestyle decisions. Making memories with my family is my priority."

—**Karmen Gearhart**, CLU, CFP®, co-founder of Kar-Mel Financial Planners

. . .

"My splurges won't derail me from my long-term goals."

—**Kathy Bazany**, Pharmacist

. . .

"I have never considered a strategy of beginning at the end of my life! If you want to live an extraordinary life, it makes sense to begin at the end. Melissa is right on track when she challenges her readers to focus on their values."

—**Tracy L. Bailey**, MBA

"As a single woman in my late 30s, I was lost about how to make financial decisions. I was envious of others who had a partner to consult with and make joint financial & life decisions. I felt alone and scared for my future financial success, until I used the tools in this book. It changed my mindset about money. Now that I've identified my values and established my priorities, I have more time for fun with friends and family, instead of unnecessarily worrying about finances."

—Rachel Williams, M.A., CCC-speech language pathologist

. . .

"I'm a female entrepreneur who invested my retirement into starting my business. I needed to seriously look at rebuilding for my future. Melissa has been absolutely wonderful in getting to know me, my needs, and comfort levels."

—Tonya Christiansen, owner of Must Love Dogs Boutique

. . .

"*Going Rogue* certainly awakens thoughts about how you want to live your life. It will help motivate you to really think about what is important for your future; you may find it isn't what you thought. After reading this book, you may plan an alternate, transformational route to a better, happier you!"

—Rachelle Osborn, MBA, technology project manager

. . .

"I feel like I'm on vacation every day."

—Rebecca Kelley, Home Efficiency Expert

. . .

"Melissa takes a heart-centered, judgment-free approach to helping women step into their financial power. Ladies, it's time to feel empowered around money and 'Going Rogue' is the way to do it!"

—Emilee Duell, R.N.

. . .

"It feels so good to spend more time with my family."

—Holly Larsen, Entrepreneur

Table of Contents

Introduction

I am so excited for you! For years I've wanted to get this information into your hands because it can— literally—change your life. I'm living proof and it's become my life's mission to teach what I've learned.

That's why I'm so passionate about empowering women with their money. I want you to experience life on your terms. While it may seem scary or overwhelming to let yourself even think about living your ultimate life, I'm here to help you because I know you can do it!

Chances are, if you've opened the cover and made it to this point, you're looking for answers to your financial questions. That's what you'll get—but I will deliver it in an interesting way.

I'll take you through my process so you can get clear about what matters most to you, realize what you can let go of, and better understand what you're capable of bringing into your life. You'll discover financial empowerment, which will help you operate your life with confidence so you can use your money in fulfilling ways.

Please understand that *Going Rogue!* isn't a book about investing. You won't find charts, graphs, and spreadsheets teaching you how to time the market, identify the next hot stock, or rebalance your portfolio. Why? Because I believe that living a wealthy life is way deeper than just your investments.

Forget about what's going on in the market, in Washington, D.C., China, or anywhere else. You have no control over any of that. I believe that investments are important, they're just not the subject of this book. My objective is to help you focus on what you can control.

Your best life requires you to focus on and control two things: Your mindset and your actions. Day in. Day out. Week after week. Year after year. Your approach to life directly impacts your results. Regardless of your monetary wealth, you can experience the joy of living a rich life when you decide what's ideal for you.

Money aside, would you agree that at the end of the day, all you really want in life is peace, love, and happiness? Aren't those the things we truly value the most?

1

INTRODUCTION

I do not believe that you have to choose between money and your values. In fact, I believe that money, when managed correctly, can be a huge advantage to living your life **more** in accordance with your values. But…money can be scary, overwhelming, and burdensome. How has the subject of money become so taboo? What is it about money that it has so much control, instead of being controlled? Why does money elicit feelings of guilt, unworthiness, shame, and even greed? It doesn't have to be this way.

Associating money with power, control, greed, growth, returns, and ego are often tied to a male-dominated financial system. These traditional financial systems in which we've been indoctrinated, leave little to no room for emotions. Decisions are made and advice is given based solely on numbers. Logic. The good ol' boys club standardized what people "should" want. Black and white. No gray areas. It seems few considerations are given to individual values, which can cause you to feel disconnected and intimidated. You may have felt like you weren't being heard even though it's YOUR money and your life.

I'll wager that at some point, tears have run down your face when you've been in a position of having to make financial decisions. I will also bet that you were frustrated by emotions of sadness, anger, or envy, and didn't understand why money stirred up so much pain. If what you've been taught about money, your personal finances, or your wealth has caused you any sort of anxiety, frustration, or concerns, and if you want to avoid regrets down the road, this is your book.

Join me on your new journey to a higher quality of life, a life packed with positive emotions! Flip the script you've been reading. Gain your new perspective. Step back and look at life from new angles. Be curious.

Going Rogue! delivers inspiration, motivation, and the framework you need so you can optimize your life, from any age, income, stage of life, or level of wealth. After all, it is YOUR life and you have my permission to do things _your_ way.

My wish for you is that you Go Rogue! May you live your ideal life and be a blessing to others.

Warmly,

YOUR VISION, YOUR REALITY

Live Your Ideal Life

CHAPTER 1

Begin at the End

For where your treasure is, there your heart will be also.
—*Matthew 6:21 (NIV)*

You might expect that a book for women about money would start out by teaching you how to create a budget or give you savvy investment strategies. Surprise, I'm Going Rogue!

Begin with the End in Mind

Fast forward to the years when you've become frail. As you reflect on your life, what will you have accomplished? Ask yourself what you'll be proud of. Consider why it will have mattered. Will you have lived relatively free of regrets?

The reason I ask you to think about what's important to your future self is, that doing so mitigates roadblocks to your success. No matter how successful you've been up to this point in your life, the experiences you've had, your limiting beliefs, biases, and the opinions of others could be holding you back from living your ideal life, for the REST of your life.

> **BE UNCONVENTIONAL:** Work backward from where you *want* to be to where you are today.

The Formula

Your quality of life and the impact you make on the world are the results of your mindset. If you want to optimize your life, for every day going forward, keep reading to find your inspiration and motivation along with strategic tools you can put to use immediately.

When you were in school, did you think it was absolutely ridiculous to learn algebra or geometry? My son feels that way right now. "When am I going to use algebra in the real world?" Like I replied to him, "You'll use algebra all the time, you just won't realize you're doing so at the time."

7

In fact, we're going to do some algebra right here, right now. "Melissa, what are you talking about? I don't want to do ANY algebra!" Don't worry, it's easy and the formula is a tool you can apply throughout your life for better outcomes in different types of situations.

Here's where the algebra comes in. You know the **event** [think of various life categories happening in your current situation or circumstance]. You know what you want as your **outcome** [result]. To get the outcome you desire, you choose your **response** [your action] to each event. In other words, the way you manage your responses—your mindset—is the single largest contributor to your results. For better outcomes, respond prudently to your circumstances.

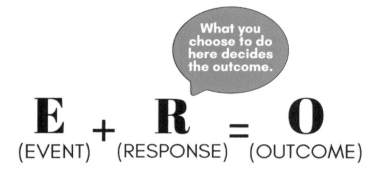

What you choose to do here decides the outcome.

$$E + R = O$$

(EVENT)   (RESPONSE)   (OUTCOME)

Stay with me, okay? I promise there won't be tons of math in this book, but there will be self-responsibility. If you want to live your ideal life and be a blessing to others, it's time to take a personal inventory of your values and priorities.

Values

Two of my core values are health and personal relationships. Another value of mine is financial stability. To build and maintain my friendships along with focusing on my health, I'll take a walk or play tennis with a friend rather than going out to a restaurant, which saves money. In this example, all three of my values have favorable results.

Of the five value areas below, what's most important to you? Rank them from 1-5 with 1 being the most important. [It's okay to write in this book as we go along.]

Value Areas

- Faith
  - Spiritual – Personal
  - Spiritual – Community

- Relationships
  - Family
  - Friends
  - Colleagues
  - Acquaintances
  - Strangers

- Health
  - Nutrition
  - Fitness
  - Mindset

- Finances
  - Career
  - Education
  - Generosity
  - Security

- Fun
  - Planned
  - Spontaneous

Does the way you live your life accurately reflect your values? Think about your day so far today. What were you doing before you started reading this chapter? Who were you with? Was the way you spent your time and money lining up with your rankings you placed above?

For better insight, take a look at your calendar and checkbook, or online banking statement, over the last month. Better yet, review your calendar and spending history over the last year. What do you notice about the ways you've spent money? Your highest priority doesn't necessarily require the most time or money. Give yourself grace if you make the observation that your money and values aren't in complete alignment.

Awareness is the first step toward lasting change.

in·ten·tion·al
in'ten(t)SH(ə)n(ə)l
An action performed with awareness,
done deliberately, consciously, on purpose.

Here's an exercise to help you find clarity regarding your money and values so that you can be more intentional with your actions. Your mindset will make a difference!

In each of your core value areas, consider what's good right now and what it is that you'd like to improve. Is there a financial connection between where you are today and what you want in the future?

I suggest you start by identifying your specific value, then the outcome you want for the future. Next, assess your situation today (or an event that could happen). Last, what is your response to make your desired outcome true?

Take a few minutes to fill in the chart below.

V VALUE (present)	E EVENT (present)	+ R RESPONSE (action)	= O OUTCOME (future)
family time	*found out I'm pre-diabetic*	*hire a trainer & nutritionist*	*possibly have more quality time with grandkids*

Or does your response look more like this because of a limiting belief?

VALUE	EVENT	RESPONSE	OUTCOME
family time	*found out I'm pre-diabetic*	*do nothing because I "can't afford it"*	*possibly limit quality time with grandkids*

If after the exercise above, you feel like you've got it pretty good, and that all of your values are reflected in your finances, I'll give you a challenge. You probably have room in your life for something bigger than anything you've ever done. It's time for a BHAG.

Wait, What's a BHAG??

For those of you wondering what a BHAG is, it stands for Big Hairy Audacious Goal. In my opinion, a BHAG should both excite you and scare you!

Some BHAGs I've accomplished include traveling around Europe for six weeks (before the internet) with only a *Let's Go: Europe* book as a reference guide; paying off my house before I was 40; and starting a business without incurring any debt. A future BHAG of mine is to complete America's Great Loop. If you've never heard of "The Loop," check it out here at **https://greatloop.org**. In a nutshell, it's a 6,000-mile boat trip around the eastern half of the United States. I'm pumped!

Here's How to Brainstorm Your BHAG (check off each as you create yours):
____ Dream Big
____ Be Open to Learning
____ Plan Early
____ Share Your Goals
____ Make Adjustments
____ Stay Focused
____ Think of it as an Adventure

Your turn. What's your Big Hairy Audacious Goal? Go ahead and write it down here. You don't need to share it with anyone, but, you'll be more likely to accomplish your goal simply because it's in writing. Ready, set, go!

_____

_____

_____

_____

_____

You can dream, design, and live your ideal life.

So, start dreaming:

✓ Don't let your limiting beliefs get in the way of what you truly want.

✓ Stop procrastinating.

✓ Do expand your spheres of influence.

✓ Go your own way!

Tune in to your feelings about your life and finances. Remember the times when you've struggled with a decision? You may well have deliberated with yourself for hours trying to figure out what you were going to do. How did it feel after you made the decision when you **knew** you made the right choice?

GO ROGUE: Your best financial decisions will make you feel good and aren't always tied to how much money you made or saved.

How do you want to **feel** when you're living your ideal life?

What feeling will you have when you:

➲ Take the next step forward in your faith.

➲ Improve or restore a personal relationship.

➲ Commit to a healthier way of living.

➲ Direct your time and money into something that's rewarding.

➲ Experience genuine FUN!!

In Chapter 2, "The Best Investment," the world needs the gifts you have inside of you. If you're unsure of how to positively impact the world, let alone your own life, or if you're questioning what your next "R" (response) should be, let people help you.

You just have to *ask*.

Let's explore the possibilities…

CHAPTER 2

The Best Investment

Whether you think you can, or you think you can't, you're right.
—Henry Ford

You might expect that with "The Best Investment" as this chapter's title, you'll get an education on investments. Or, tips of the trade on how to get rich in the stock market. I'm Going Rogue! You'll learn about the best investment you can make, but it's not what you think.

Mindset

If you want something different or better in your life, do something to affect change. Excuses won't help you. Belief in yourself will. Confidence to embrace opportunities comes from self-knowledge. We've been told to study hard, get good grades, go to college, work hard, and save your money so you can retire someday.

However, it wasn't only about working and saving when Darcy landed her first job. Instead, her parents encouraged her to follow her North Star. Establish a strong financial foundation **and** enjoy the journey of life. She took charge, put money into retirement, bought a home and a reliable car, paid cash for purchases, and invested in herself to further her career. Instead of being focused on promotions for the sake of an increased salary, Darcy has centered her attention on adding value in whatever position she holds and is confident that the money will follow. She works because it's a labor of love, not a labor of finances.

Do you love your career? What would need to happen to make it even better?

_____

_____

What are you going to change so that you can love your career?

_____

_____

Start making wise choices

Choose...

√	A POSITIVE MINDSET
√	TO LEARN
√	TO GET OUT OF YOUR COMFORT ZONE
√	EMBRACE FAILURE
√	TO HELP
√	TO OPTIMIZE
√	TO THRIVE

Have you ever said something that sounds like this, "If I just had more money, everything would be okay"?

Money is NOT the solution to your issues in life. The way you **think** about the challenges in your life is your game changer. Before we move on, you get to dream. Dream big. Ready? Please give serious consideration to this question:

How much money would it take to completely change your life?

Let's say that you just received a one-time unexpected sum of money. Would $20 change your life? How about:

$200?

$2,000?

$20,000?

$200,000?

$2 million?

$20 million+?

Circle your answer in the list above.

While a one-time, life-changing windfall might be nice, nearly 100% percent of the women I interviewed for this book stated that the most important thing about money was security. You feel secure when there's money in the bank and enough money coming in so that you can maintain your life$tyle. You feel secure when you're able to provide for yourself and not burden others. Money gives you freedom to make your own choices, travel, give, and enjoy life.

Yet, money tends to be a source of stress and frustration. How much money would you need to have to eliminate your stresses and frustrations? Lump sum or annual income, how much would it take to improve your quality of life? Don't settle. Go after it! You have the capacity to bring forth major change and optimize your life. Don't make the mistake of "just keeping up" and don't fall into the trap of accepting that things are "just the way they are." You can choose your mindset and your future.

BE UNCONVENTIONAL: The best way to transform your income is to invest in yourself.

You are Always Investing

Time, money, emotional energy. What are you doing to invest in yourself? The investments you make in yourself allow you to accomplish more and have reserves of time, money, and emotional energy to give to others.

17

Education

I'm a life-long learner. I love to read and always have. In high school, one of my teachers would let us have trivia day on occasional Fridays. At that point in my life, I hadn't traveled anywhere, yet I knew most of the geography answers because of all the reading I'd done. It was interesting, years later, when I did begin to travel, I felt connected to cities like New York and Paris, like I'd been there before. I believe it's because I had read so many books and learned about those cities before having experienced them.

My personal belief is that every one of us should always be learning. Formal or informal education is preparation for what lies before us. Just remember that the difference between knowledge and transformation is the action you take. Increase your knowledge AND take action.

Challenge yourself to learn something new every day. A fact, a word, a word in another language, a new idea, or how to do something. Turn off the noise. Quiet yourself. Tap into your intelligence.

What are you grateful for?

_____

_____

What are your talents and skills?

_____

_____

What brings you joy?

_____

_____

What do you want to get done? When?

_____

_____

What's standing between you and your accomplishments?

_____

_____

Your achievements are just a resource away. Higher education may be necessary, but there are numerous low- and no-cost resources available to you right now. All it takes is for you to start seeking those avenues. What's available online? In your community? Hey, the library is still an option! Rachel Hollis built a multi-million-dollar business with a high school degree and shares that everything she's learned, she learned for free.

Who do you know? Someone wants to help you and will be able to point you in the right direction. I'm someone. How about investing 10 seconds of your time to schedule your free 15-minute phone or Zoom call with me so we can brainstorm.

 **Phone or Zoom.**
Schedule your
FREE 15-minute call
with Melissa Myers

https://go.oncehub.com/MelissaMyers

Know Thyself

Socrates is the philosopher who said, "Know thyself." When you truly understand yourself, you recognize your value. You're then in a position to make prioritized actions. Remember, **you** have God-given ability and power to make a different way for yourself. If higher education is required, don't let money or your age be an excuse.

> *Don't let anyone tell you that you have to pay for higher education.*
> *There's always a way for someone else to pay for you.*
> —Marilyn A.

19

Action

It's never too late to invest in yourself and you can take as much time as you need. Dawn, a working mom and wife, chose to further her education when she was in her early 30s. At the age of 44, after having taken breaks for her hubby's health issues and then her own, she earned her bachelor's degree. Her degree didn't cost her a dime, only her time, because she utilized her employer-sponsored tuition reimbursement program.

Armed with an education and ambition, her income has tripled because she pursued projects, leadership roles, and promotions. Dawn has no regrets about spending the necessary time away from her family to earn her degree because her education has changed her life. She put herself out there, accepted challenges, and followed through. Now she has more time and money for the people she cares about!

Your turn. Multiply your income by three:

$_____ × 3 = $_____.

How would your life change if your income tripled?

I would go   _____

I would give   _____

I would see   _____

I would feel   _____

I would pay   _____

I would buy   _____

Initiative, not a college degree, transformed Mary's life. Some of Mary's earliest memories are of working in the fields and orchards with her parents. As forward thinkers, they encouraged her to complete high school because they knew it was essential for a better paying job and a better life. After graduation, Mary began working in a migrant agency as a bilingual clerk. Just as her dad taught himself how to read and speak English, Mary embraced opportunities to learn.

When her office got their first computer, she learned how to use it and became the go-to resource in the office. With each new job and role, she took the initiative to learn, which led to more occasions for education and self-devel-

opment. Her strong work ethic opened doors to leadership roles that required her to speak in front of large groups, which helped her get over her shyness. As Mary did, I encourage you to spend time learning because your knowledge and application will lead to opportunities from which you'll benefit in and outside of the workplace!

YOU are the best investment ever!

Believe in yourself.

✓ Start investing in yourself.

✓ Don't settle for less and don't settle for just keeping up.

✓ Stop telling yourself lies.

✓ Do more soul searching.

✓ Go outside your comfort zone.

You can **GO ROGUE**! Take imperfect action toward your dreams, no matter your age or financial status. Choose a can-do mindset. Yearn to learn. Apply your knowledge. Learn from your mistakes. You can do anything you want. I believe in you!

When you invest in yourself, you can be more generous. That's what I'll share in Chapter 3, "Start Giving."

CHAPTER 3

Start Giving

From everyone who has been given much,
much will be demanded; and from the
one who has been entrusted with much,
much more will be asked.
—Luke 12:48 (NIV)

You might expect that this chapter, "Start Giving," with a verse like Luke 12:48 following the title, would be written for the woman who has more money than she needs, or that this chapter is about tithing and ways to increase your itemized tax deductions. I'm Going Rogue!

The "Domino Effect" Intrigues Me

When I reflect on my life, I'm acutely aware of the acts of kindness bestowed on me by others. They've triggered a chain reaction that has brought me to this exact moment in time, when I'm writing this book, this chapter, for you.

At this stage I can wholeheartedly say I'm a responsible manager of my finances, but that wasn't always the case. In my early 20s, I was a server at a nice restaurant. The assistant manager expected me to know wine basics, but in the beginning, I didn't. When I confused Cabernet with Chardonnay, she became upset with me. I like to make everyone happy, so to avoid facing my mistake, along with future pain and conflict, I decided I wasn't going to go back to work there. Ever. I was a no-show for my next shift.

Luckily for me, Becky, the General Manager, sought me out and helped me mature. She gave me a second chance, which was a life-changing blessing! It was because I was able to continue working there, that I became friends with another server, Kristen, who later introduced me to a career as a financial advisor. This career changed my life and gives me opportunities to help others transform their own lives.

Generosity, acts of kindness, cause-based giving, and paying it forward create life-altering, ripple effects that positively impact the world. Without even realizing it or ever knowing the outcome, you are making an impact.

Twenty-some years ago, Becky had no idea that her act of kindness would result in my helping you live your ideal life. She couldn't have guessed that I'd be writing this book, let alone be in a position to donate all of its proceeds to non-profits that serve women.

When you give, you change lives and the world.

We All Have Something to Give

How and what to give is not isolated to financial gifts. The act of giving can be intentional, impulsive, or in response to a situation. If you've been wanting to give and were unsure about where, when, or how to give, keep reading!

Everyone has something to give. You can give your time, talent and expertise, or treasure (money). You can give upon your passing, during your life, or both. In Chapter 1, I encouraged you to look back on your life and consider what it is that you'll be proud of and why what you did will have mattered. Will you want to have had more time or more money?

**Fill needs individually or as a group,
big or small with time or money.**

Time

I believe that time is more valuable than money. Time is a currency. Whatever it is that you're doing, you're paying with time. Your cost is what you give up. You give up other activities, rest, and spending time with people who are important to you.

However, the time you give up doesn't have to be anything more than a few seconds. Start smiling! Smiles and hugs are free and make everyone feel better. Simple gestures matter. A handwritten note or a phone call can change some-one's day. Giving is more than just financially.

Volunteering your time is another great way to give. When you make the choice to give of yourself, it doesn't have to be a long-term obligation. You can give your time by volunteering at a single event, or you can make an ongoing

commitment. When you make the decision to volunteer, do a quick self-check to make sure your values and the mission of the organization are in alignment.

> *Get involved with local government so you*
> *know what's going on in your own community.*
> —Jackie R.

The more you know, the better prepared you'll be to give back. Your local government, non-profits, and churches have needs and you could be the one who provides some of the needed resources because of your time and knowledge. When you understand what is going on in your backyard, you can make valuable contributions by connecting people and resources to the cause.

Random acts of kindness are another way to give your time. Be observant. If you see needs, fill them. For example, a New Yorker noticed us Midwesterners huddled around the subway map. It was obvious that we were clueless. He asked us where we were heading, then explained how to navigate the subway so we could get to the restaurant downtown. His random act of kindness changed my opinion of New Yorkers.

Modeling Kindness and Generosity

A few years ago, my son and I were driving home from vacation. As we took the final exit ramp after hours on the road, I noticed a vehicle that appeared to be coasting to a stop. Sensing something was wrong, I pulled up to the car and rolled down the window, keeping distance for safety. "Are you okay?" I asked the driver. He replied that he'd run out of gas. There was a gas station just up the road, so I told him I'd be happy to go get gas for him. He said he didn't have any cash on him. "No worries. I'll be right back," I said with a smile and drove off. When we returned with a full gas can, he expressed his gratitude. I'm not sure who was happier, him or us!

Talent and Expertise

Marilyn shares her expertise through one-to-one mentoring with young women who have chosen engineering careers.

Meghan has a talent for teaching women how to "fish" by giving them the opportunity to acquire experience so they gain confidence, which leads to massive life transformations. I've applied my personal and professional experiences with money as a volunteer in my church's financial literacy programs.

Cara, an estate planning attorney, serves on the boards of half a dozen non-profits. Giving back to the community, she performs her duties as a board member and is a valuable resource, able to offer her legal expertise as situations warrant.

Do you have an idea, product, or service that you know would help others, but have an inner conflict because you would profit from it? My business coach, Robyn Crane, created FEMM, Female Empowered Money Makers, a mentorship program designed for women in service-based businesses. Over time, FEMM evolved and primarily serves female financial advisors.

Robyn's mission is to see the financial services industry changed for the better by more women getting in and staying in the industry. She believes that with more women in financial services, more clients will get the support they need and more lives will be changed for the better. For Robyn, *It's all about changing lives.*

What if you began to think of money as a tool that can be used for goodness in the world, rather than allow it to hold you back, or make you feel guilty or ashamed? If you can improve the lives of others, and you stand to profit from it, don't let the money that you could make stop you. After all, the more money you make, the more you can give.

Think about it this way. What you start could give hope to someone who needs hope. A job to someone who wants to work. A fresh start. A second chance. These opportunities will create a ripple effect that positively impact lives for generations. If your heart is right, I believe it is perfectly fine to make money from your ideas.

Create, design, and innovate. Use your talents to make a positive impact. What talents and expertise do you bring to the table that could benefit your community? The world?

Remember, we all have something to give and your ability to give something isn't isolated to your finances. You can give of your talents and areas of expertise.

Treasure

The Bible teaches us to give of our income—the "first fruits" that come into our household. If you're a Christian, tithing to your church could be your launching point for giving. For me, tithing is an act of faith. I release control and trust that the money I give will be properly managed for the benefit of others.

Being Mindful and Intentional

If you're not tithing, there are plenty of other ways to start giving or to increase your level of financial support. What causes are on your mind? What atrocities break your heart? Getting clear on these questions will help you decide where, when, and how to give.

> *Meaningful, caused-based gifts*
> *of time or money bring blessings,*
> *and the blessings aren't just for you.*

Before any form of giving, take a moment to pray and rest in faith that your gift will bless others. For example, when you declutter your home and drop off everything at the resale shop, offer up a prayer that your donation is a blessing.

It can be as simple as sharing extras of something you have with strangers. Melanie is observant and looks for opportunities to share her store coupons inside places like Banana Republic and Victoria's Secret. On one shopping trip with her daughters, she handed a bunch of coupons to the man waiting in the checkout line, his arms overflowing with special lingerie for his wife. He was clearly uncomfortable shopping in such a feminine store and the coupons helped break the ice. He relaxed and was extremely grateful for the significant savings, all because of a stranger's gift of coupons.

Here's an idea to try in your home. When you get solicitations in the mail asking for your financial support, hold a charitable giving committee meeting. Bring all household members together to review the various asks. Allow time for questions and to hear each other's thoughts on which organizations you'll give to and at what level. It's something you can incorporate into your schedule, maybe once a month or quarter. It's an intentional practice that is mindful and a great way to model generosity. There's also another bonus: More family time!

Regardless of which school or organization is selling, when a kid knocks on my door selling fundraiser coupon books, I buy. My purchase helps the organization and honors the businesses who sponsored the book. The student learns communication skills through the sales process and gains self-confidence and leadership skills. When friends and family are over at my house, I offer them the coupons of their choice. Coupons aren't a huge financial gift, but they are an all-around win for everyone!

You can get creative with ways to be intentional with your giving plan. Being mindful of needs versus wants, I chose to give up professional manicures and pedicures for an entire year. It was one of the ways I was able to "level up" my charitable giving. After eliminating a cost, you could then choose to redirect that monthly payment to a worthy cause. I know of a couple who, after they paid off their mortgage, redirected the monthly mortgage payment to a missionary, giving their ministry a pledge to do so for one year. How cool is that?

Many of you want to give and are waiting to make sure you're financially set first. If you want to feel more confident about your financial ability to give or if you would like ideas on various gifting strategies, seek professional advice so that you have clarity about your situation and your possibilities.

Your team of planners, including your accountant, attorney, insurance agent, and financial planner, are there to help you in your giving plans. You may be surprised to learn that you could leave a legacy by gifting your property for conservation, protecting it from development. Or, that there are strategies you could use to keep your family cottage in the family, with little to no out-of-pocket cost to your family.

Women Who Care

Think your financial gift wouldn't be large enough to have an impact? Underestimating the breadth and depth of your potential gift can actually hurt others because the people who will benefit most wouldn't be getting the resources they need. Let's consider the impact that $100 and 100 women can make in a community.

Worldwide, there are chapters of 100+ women who meet quarterly and make a group gift to a local nonprofit. Here's how it works. The meeting is only an hour

and there are no attendance requirements. If you are unable to attend, you just mail a check. Easy. Time isn't going to keep you from participating.

At the meeting, women interested in speaking on behalf of a nonprofit put their names in the hat. Three names are drawn. One at a time, each of the three women speaks for five minutes, sharing what their organization is all about and how the funds would be used if they were selected as the winning organization. They then have five minutes to answer questions from the audience members.

Individually, members vote for the nonprofit to which they would like the proceeds to be donated. While the votes are being tallied, the winning organization from the previous meeting shares what they've done with the funds, how the money has impacted their cause, and the lives that have been touched. After the presentation, the winner is announced and attendees write their checks for $100 to the winning nonprofit.

> **BE UNCONVENTIONAL:** The concept of multiplication with
> **$100 X 100 women = $10,000** is possible where YOU live.
> Think big and create something similar to meet a need.

If you'd like to participate in this type of giving circle, join a local chapter of Women Who Care or start one in your community. Here is a link to my chapter's Facebook page: **http://tiny.cc/Tri-CityWomenWhoCare**.

The Hope Project USA

Started in 2006 as a faith-based outreach program to educate and inform the community about the issue of human trafficking, The Hope Project provide healing for girls and women who have survived sex trafficking. They are now in the process of opening a home in West Michigan for girls ages 11-17, where they will provide comprehensive services to address the physical, mental, emotional, and spiritual aspects of recovery.

Human trafficking breaks my heart. When I learned of The Hope Project USA, I became a regular monthly supporter and have committed 100% of the proceeds from the launch of this book to the organization. To learn more, visit their website at **https://www.hopeprojectusa.org**. If you'd like to join me with your financial support, you can click "Get Involved" and then "Give."

Giving as a Way of Life

Be a Changemaker

In my interview with Kirsten Bunch, Founder of Women's Changemaker Mentorship™ and the international bestselling author of *Next Act, Give Back*, she shared how she works with women who have a voice inside their hearts telling them that they can do more. Her recommendation—whether you are working, retired, widowed, or divorced—is to let curiosity open doors in discovering where your money can do the most good.

Kirsten said, "Curiosity is a great way to get over fear." As you're exploring causes to champion, "Pay attention. If you're uncomfortable, don't be afraid to have conversations." You can be a changemaker and make a real difference. Kirsten challenges all of us, "Don't have the confidence? Just do it anyway."

Look for Opportunities: Think, Ask, Act

Oftentimes, it's simply being cognizant of those around us. Observing a situation where you can "give" doesn't always require money.

There was a man on one of those motorized scooters in the grocery store looking up at the top shelf of products. I'm **THINK**ing it's going to be challenging for him to grab what he needed, so I just **ASK**ed him, "Can I get that for you?" Asking permission is important because some people don't want help, but don't let a "no" dissuade you from asking the next time. I think that having a servant mentality in offering to be of assistance and **ACT**ing on it connects us with people. I don't want to miss those moments that make someone's day and give me joy.

Give Back by Paying it Forward

Perhaps you've overcome a really bad situation that required the financial and emotional support of others. You're not alone. Many women have been in horrible relationships without access to, or control over, their finances. When they needed to leave, the only way out was to ask friends for a place to stay.

Many women have been in the position of needing to ask friends for money for attorney fees to start the divorce process. Now on the other side, many of these women are ready to help a fellow sister with cash, meals, a safe place, or whatever she needs. They know what it takes because they've been there. They mentor, lend an ear, make introductions, and help their friend make the move, sometimes literally moving that friend out of the toxic environment. They've joined together to create support groups and have established funding resources to assist women who need to leave and find a place to go.

If you need to get out, please do it now. Don't let a lack of resources keep you from seeking safety. Help is available; you just need to ask. Ask a friend, your church, or a woman's organization in your community. For anyone who thinks they may need to leave in the future, and has the time and ability to plan, it's recommended to have $10,000 on hand. You can regroup on much less and in some parts of the country it could take a lot more, but $10,000 is the number that comes up in conversations about starting over.

Create and Leave a Legacy

You can start small or go big. Whether you want to help another woman get back on her own two feet, further her education, or contribute to preserving and conserving our planet, there are ways to make an impact during your life, upon your passing, or both. Legacy is about taking action—often a series of actions, over time. Actions that when added up, make a significant and lasting impact. Sometimes for generations.

While education is one of my top values, I wish I'd known about alternatives to getting an education without accumulating student loan debt. I know first-hand how difficult it can be to get out from under the weight of student loans and how the debt holds you back. It was a financial burden I carried into my 30s. Not wanting that same burden for others, I decided to do my part to help women (adults and those right out of high school) get their degrees with minimal or no student loans.

I established a **scholarship fund** with the Grand Haven Area Community Foundation. The fund started small with my initial contribution, but over time it's grown and will continue to grow throughout my life as I make periodic additions. My ask is that when I pass, memorial gifts be given to my scholarship fund in lieu of flowers.

Melissa Skiera Myers Scholarship Fund
https://ghacf.org/scholarships/scholarship-funds

You can do something similar or just regularly give to a scholarship program of your choice that's already in place.

Mastermind with Women Who Give

There is power in collaboration, so start conversations about your intentions. You never know what can happen! If you're unsure about getting involved in your community or cause, ask your friends and family for ideas. Likely, they'll have insights that will get you moving in the right direction.

MA$TERMIND
with Women who GIVE

more people benefit

more $

more ideas

Your generous spirit helped make this book possible. Hundreds of you shared your time, stories, and opinions with me. Collectively, you gave me and each other a special gift. Many of you went outside your comfort zone and because you did, you gave me accountability to finish what I started. More importantly, you gave to women who are searching for answers, seeking inspiration, and motivation.

The BE Event, a West Michigan nonprofit organization, was founded as a way to shine a light on women by bringing women together for community and empowerment. It's all about serving and celebrating each other while giving attendees time to conduct a self-inventory and set goals for personal growth.

Ticket proceeds from the event help women in need in the local community. Founder Meghan Heritage keeps The BE Event community informed about how "we" have made our sisters' lives better. We've helped women get their cars repaired and buy tires, pay funeral bills, utility and medical bills, buy food and diapers, and more.

Fundraising

Social media and direct mail campaigns are effective ways for nonprofits to raise funds. However, when asked about your charitable giving decisions, many of you said that a personal ask carries a lot more weight than making the decision to respond to something in the mail, on TV, or online. It can be scary to ask for money, but when you volunteer to raise money for a cause, trust that you'll be helping the organization achieve results by making a personal ask. Keep in mind who will benefit from the generosity of donors. Isn't your organization and its mission worth a bit of discomfort?

GO ROGUE: If you have time, knowledge, or money that can make someone's life better, give even if you profit from it! Don't let fears of self-promotion hold you back. Solve problems. Create opportunities. Design. Innovate. Make a positive impact. Be a blessing.

Who can you bless with the gift of a second chance?

_____

_____

Time is short. How can you use your time today to make someone's day better?

_____

_____

What time, talent, or treasure can you give for the benefit of planet earth?

_____

_____

Chapter 4, "Don't Start with a Budget," will help you analyze your life$tyle and give you a new awareness into your ability to be generous financially.

YOUR FINANCIAL GPS
Enjoy the Journey

Don't Start with a Budget

Be sure you know the condition of your flocks,
give careful attention to your herds;
for riches do not endure forever,
and a crown is not secure for all generations.
—*Proverbs 27:23-24 (NIV)*

Conventional wisdom will tell you that when it's time to get your finances in order, the place to start is with a budget. I actually don't recommend that. Instead, I'm Going Rogue!

You probably already know that it's wise to:

- Live on less than you make
- Pay yourself first
- Invest for retirement
- Get the right types of insurance
- Pay down debt
- Have an emergency fund

If you know WHAT to do, yet get stuck on HOW, this chapter is for you! The reason why I advise you to NOT start with the task of creating a budget is that there are a lot of moving parts to budgeting and there's a common tendency to make unrealistic budgets. Lack of clarity about your spending will set you up for failure with a budget that's overly restrictive and doesn't account for life events. How many times have you heard someone say, "I've tried budgeting, but budgets don't work for me?"

What not to do as your first step:

➲ DON'T start by trying to create a budget
➲ DON'T start investing
➲ DON'T start paying extra on your debt

But aren't all these things—creating a budget, investing, and paying down debt—things I should be doing to help me improve my finances? While those are good actions to take, they might not be the **best** first step.

My objective is to help you win with your finances by teaching you a path to your Passport to Freedom! It's an easy-to-implement, step-by-step process:

1. Get organized
2. Calculate your net worth
3. Check your credit
4. Analyze your life$tyle
5. Reduce debt
6. Build and protect your wealth

Download your **BONUS** *Passport to Freedom* companion workbook, so that you have the template for each concept discussed in this chapter.

Download your
FREE BONUS
Passport to Freedom Workbook
passport.askmelissamyers.com

Get Organized

What do you own?

Collect your account statements:

- Bank and/or credit union accounts
- Investment accounts
- Cash value life insurance

Check to find if you have:
- Savings bonds
- Stock certificates
- Good old cash—count it all, even the money in your change jar!
- Gift cards

What else do you own:
- Home
- Vehicles
- Other things with motors
- Jewelry
- Art
- High-end electronics
- Firearms
- Collectibles/Antiques
- Real estate
- A business
- Intellectual property

What do you owe?
- Car loans
- Loans on things with motors
- Credit cards
- Student loans
- Medical bills
- Mortgage
- Personal loans from friends and family
- Bills in collections

Calculate Your Net Worth

Grab a pen, sheet of paper, and a calculator. Write the word "ASSETS" (what you own) at the top of the page and list everything you own and the value of each; then add up the total. [Or, utilize the Net Worth page in your companion workbook.]

If you have no idea how much something is worth, use your best judgment. You can guesstimate. How much could you reasonably get if you sold that item? Or think about it this way: How much would you pay if you were to buy that item today? Still stuck? There's always Google.

Next, create a new page titled "LIABILITIES" (what you owe) and record the name of the debt and amount for each of these items. Total your debt. If you don't have any debt, write a big, fat zero under Liabilities. (BTW…Congratulations!!!)

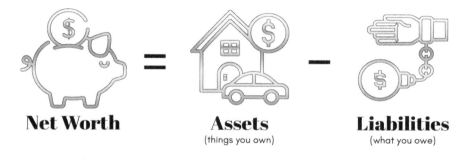

Net Worth   **Assets**   **Liabilities**
(things you own)   (what you owe)

Your net worth is a simple formula that can help you understand your financial situation. After you've totaled your assets and totaled your liabilities, the final step is to subtract your liabilities from your assets. The answer is your Net Worth.

In your BONUS *Passport to Freedom* workbook, you'll find the Net Worth template shown on the opposite page.

NET WORTH

Net worth is a measure of your financial strength. As you start calculating and tracking your net worth from year to year, set an annual goal for yourself. How much do you want to grow your net worth this year? In five years? Ten? The larger your net worth, the more choices and freedoms you have.

ASSETS

Collect your account statements:	VALUE
Bank and/or Credit Union account total	
Investment Accounts total	
Cash Value Life Insurance	
Do you have:	
Savings bonds	
Stock certificates	
Good old cash. (Count it all, even the money in your change jar!)	
Gift Cards	
What else do you own?	
Home value	
Vehicles value	
Other things with motors value	
Jewelry value	
Collectibles/Antiques value	
Real Estate value	
Business value	
Intellectual Property value	
ASSETS TOTAL	

LIABILITIES

What do you owe?	BALANCE
Mortgage	
Vehicle Loans	
Loans on other things with motors	
Credit Card debt total	
Student loans	
Medical Bills	
Personal loans from family and friends	
Bills in collections	
LIABILITIES TOTAL	

ASSETS		–	**LIABILITIES**		=	**NET WORTH**	

43

Why Is Net Worth Important?

The higher your net worth, the better prepared you'll be to embrace opportunities that come your way. Your net worth gives you freedoms and increases your ability to give to and bless others. Opportunities to build your net worth are everywhere, you just need to look for them and make wise choices. You may find opportunities in…

Real Estate

Real estate and retirement accounts are typically the two largest assets in your portfolio. Making wise real estate purchases, in other words, buying it right (not overpaying), can boost your net worth significantly over time. Would you like to own a better home? Purchase a second home? Buy a rental or a commercial property?

Career

The more financially secure you are, the more prepared you'll be to quit your job, take a different job, or become self-employed. A side benefit of growing your net worth is that the higher it is, the less financial risk you have if you get downsized or change careers.

Life Experiences

A positive net worth enables you to create life experiences in line with your values for you and your family. Many families are shifting away from giving gifts to giving experiences. What kind of memories could your net worth create?

Early Retirement

Dreaming of an early retirement? What will it take? Income to have the life$tyle you desire, right? Plan early and often with your financial planner and accountant for strategies that utilize your net worth to produce income. The strategies could include a combination of spending your nest egg and using it to produce residual or passive income. There are opportunities to turn your dreams into your reality.

Leverage

The larger your net worth, the more leverage you have. Leverage enables you to use the equity in something you already own to help finance the purchase of something else.

Leverage *can* get you into trouble. Big Trouble. Exercise caution and prudence when using it. For example, let's say you used the equity in your home to buy another piece of property, then lost your job or had a health crisis and couldn't pay your mortgage—you could lose your home to fore-closure. Be very careful with leverage!!

Cash Purchases

If you seek safety over leverage, pay cash. In the next chapter, I'll share ideas on how to make sound cash purchases. I've paid cash for my last four vehicles and love not having a car payment.

Generosity

Are there causes to which you'd like to donate money now, upon your passing, or both? The higher your net worth, the more generous you can be with your giving. In addition to financial gifts, you can give more of your time, talent, and expertise.

Net Worth Q&A

"How often should I calculate my net worth?"

Once a year is fine. Set a recurring event on your online calendar with no end-date. Schedule your net worth calculation for a day that is easy to remember like New Year's Day or your birthday. It doesn't matter what day of the year, just pick a date and make it an annual recurrence. Record your net worth in a place where you can easily find it like a physical file folder, e-file, spreadsheet, or Word document so you can see your progress over time.

MY NET WORTH

YEAR	2021	2022	2023	2024	2025
	$x	$xx	$xxx	$xxxx	$xxxxx

"How do I increase my net worth?"

Growing your net worth takes discipline and intentionality. Frugality, saving, investing, and paying down debt are key principles for building wealth. To increase your overall net worth, spend less than you earn, save for the expected and unexpected, have proper insurance in place, and make wise investments.

"Why should I track my net worth?"

When you track your net worth, you'll start to make better financial decisions consciously and subconsciously. Tracking your net worth gives you confirmation of how both your subliminal and conscious choices have produced results. Like a scale tells you if you're losing or gaining weight, tracking your net worth keeps you accountable to your choices.

Net Worth Goals

Here are several examples:

➢ "Change negative net worth to positive net worth within three years."
➢ "Grow net worth by $200,000 over the next five years."
➢ "Achieve a net worth of $1,000,000 by the age of 40."

Get uncomfortable. Remember BHAGs? Your goals should make you a little uncomfortable. Set goals that require you to stretch. Ditch the words "more" or "less" or "some" when goal setting. Instead, use a **SMART** goal framework like this to create your goals. Be:

❂ **Specific**
❂ **Measurable**
❂ **Achievable**
❂ **Relevant**
❂ Established with a **Timeframe**

I'm a big believer in posting your goals in a visible location and sharing them with an accountability partner.

Without accountability, it's easy to give up.

Get Goaling!

Use this space to record your net worth goal.

_____

_____

If you're ready to improve your financial condition, don't, I repeat **don't start by making a budget**. Rather, determine your financial baseline by calculating your net worth.

Credit

After you've calculated your net worth, the next step is to know where you stand regarding your credit. Beyond knowing your **credit score**, look at your **credit report** to find out if anyone has fraudulently used your identity to obtain credit. Review your credit report for mistakes and inaccuracies. Debt is easy to get into and hard to get out of, so look at your report to find out if you have any credit messes that need to be cleaned up.

I don't even want to think about it right now, might be surfacing in your mind. I encourage you to have a new mantra: "The longer I wait, the longer it'll take." There is a real cost of procrastination, and it isn't just a financial cost. There are emotional and relational costs too. What excuses are you holding on to? What excuses are you ready to let go of?

I've been watching my credit score and it's improving. Plus, I'm investing and getting a match from my employer so I should be good, right? My suggestion is that you change how you measure "good". Instead of using your credit score as a measure of your financial health, I recommend using your net worth as the indicator. You still need to know your credit score and what's on your credit report, but those are indicators of how often you borrow money and how good you are about paying it back. Net worth tells you how good you are about accumulating wealth. The more wealth you have, the less debt you'll need.

A low credit score can cost you with higher interest rates on loans or by being denied credit. As part of routine background checks, potential employers often check your credit. Insurance companies base their rates, in part, on your credit score. Looking to rent? Be prepared, landlords check credit, too.

Victim beware: Identity theft is real. If you didn't make a mess of your credit and someone else did, you'll need to take personal initiative to resolve the fraudulent uses of your credit. That probably sounds like it will be boring. Yes, it will be. What will be exciting, though, is watching your credit score improve. Patience. It takes time, but you can improve your credit score.

You may have heard that checking your credit will hurt your credit score. There are two types of credit score inquiries: Hard and soft. Hard inquiries affect your score because it indicates your intent to take on new credit, a risk to the creditor, especially if you're applying for credit from multiple sources. Soft inquiries, like pulling your own credit report or checking your own credit score, won't have a negative impact on your score.

Included in your **FREE *Passport to Freedom* download**, you'll walk through the steps to get your credit reports from all three credit bureaus and your credit scores. There are several credit score companies with FICO® and VantageScore® among the most popular. Generally, a high score with one credit score company means your credit score will be high with another, but it probably won't be identical due to the scoring criteria for each company.

I propose that you reframe how financial success is measured. Let's make net worth the primary measure of your financial success and include credit score as a secondary measure. Are you game?

If you want to grow your net worth, start tracking it on a regular basis, understand your motivation for increasing your wealth, and hire a CERTIFIED FINANCIAL PLANNER™ to help you. Paying your bills on time and reducing debt will help you improve your credit score. Use a calendar system to remind you to check both your net worth and credit score once a year.

Life$tyle Analysis

Have you ever considered the cost of your life$tyle today or what it will cost to have the life$tyle you want in the future? No matter what stage of life you're in, there's a cost beyond your basic needs. Your life$tyle will change over time, but you probably don't want to default into a life$tyle that isn't of your design. Your ideal life includes having choices, freedoms, independence, and opportunities.

Choices might include:

❖ Education costs

❖ Wedding(s)

❖ Buying a home

❖ Home improvements

❖ A new car

❖ Travel

❖ Investment properties

❖ Buying a vacation home

❖ Philanthropy

❖ Visiting friends, family, and grandchildren

❖ Enjoying new experiences

❖ Pursuing hobbies

❖ Buying toys (a boat, motorhome, plane, etc.)

Dreaming and setting goals for yourself can be fun but be careful. Rather than living for today without concern for the future, plan for potential risks, then go about enjoying your life. When you're clear on your current and future financial requirements, you'll minimize the degree to which you experience anxiety and fear of not having enough money.

Plan for:

❖ Emergencies

❖ Insurance deductibles and copays

❖ Out-of-pocket medical costs

❖ Insurance premiums

❖ Property taxes

❖ Pet expenses

❖ Home and vehicle maintenance

Current Expenses

To prepare for the future, you'll need clarity about the present. I believe this exercise is the single best action you can take with your money because it's the truth about your spending patterns, good and bad. In addition to what you've spent, what have you saved, invested, and given? What's on your credit card statements, bank account transactions, Venmo, PayPal, and Amazon accounts? How much money have you spent in the last week?

Next, be sure you have downloaded your **Passport to Freedom companion workbook**, which includes a template for your Life$tyle Analysis. The best way to understand what you've spent is to account for both your regular, recurring expenses as well as your infrequent expenses over longer periods of time.

While some may have differing opinions about what's essential and what's discretionary, generally you can think of your essential expenses as those for housing and utilities, food (groceries, not restaurants), transportation, insurance, saving and investing, giving, and debt repayment. Anything else is probably a discretionary expense. Think of needs versus wants.

After you've assigned categories to each of your expenses, ask yourself what changes you could make to improve your day-to-day finances. Unsure of how to categorize an expense? Refer to the "Life$tyle Analysis" worksheet in your *Passport to Freedom* workbook for ideas (a sample is shown on the opposite page).

Amazon is not a category. Open Amazon and click on "Your Orders" for an itemized listing of your purchases so you can put expense categories on what you've bought. Start categorizing your expenses from the last week, the last month, and the last three months.

After you've assigned categories to each expense, add up the totals for each category. Now divide by three. This gives you your three-month average expenses per category. A three-month average is important because it gives you a more realistic perspective on your spending. You'll pick up more of your random expenses, which are easy to forget because they aren't recurring. If you have the time and inclination, it's ideal to look at your expenses over an entire year.

LIFE$TYLE ANALYSIS

How much does your lifestyle cost you? To get a general idea, average your last 3 months of spending using the categories below. For extra clarity and extra credit, average the last 12 months of spending. Be sure to look at bank transactions, credit cards, Venmo and don't forget Amazon purchases!

ESSENTIAL

Housing	
Mortgage/Rent	
Property Taxes Winter _____ /12= _____	
Property Taxes Summer _____ /12= ___	
Total Housing	
Utilities	
Gas	
Electric	
Phone/Cable/Internet	
Cell Phone	
Garbage	
Water	
Total Utilities	

Groceries (food, toiletries, cleaning supplies, etc.)	
Transportation	
Vehicle Payment	
Gas	
Maintenance	
License Plate Tag Renewal ___ /12= ___	
Total Transportation	
Quarterly Estimated Tax (divide by 3)	
Total Credit Card Minimum Payments	
Student Loan Minimum Payments	

Insurance Premiums	
Health	
Life	
Disability (short & long term)	
Long Term Care	
Home/Umbrella	
Auto	
Total Insurance Premiums	
Misc. Health Expenses (co-pays, deductibles, prescriptions)	
Vision	
Dental	
401 K Loan Payments	
Other:	
TOTAL ESSENTIAL	

DISCRETIONARY

Giving (tithes/donations)	
Self-development	
Saving/Investing	
Personal Care (hair, massage, nails)	
Spending money/ Entertainment	
Gym	

Dining out	
Vacations	
Pet (food, vet, grooming, preventatives)	
Gifts	
Housekeeping	
Snow/Yard	

Decorating/Maintenance	
Clothing	
Dry Cleaning/Alterations	
Other:	
TOTAL DISCRETIONARY	

ESSENTIAL & DISCRETIONARY COMBINED [   ]

Infrequent Expenses

Expenses that are infrequent can wreak havoc on your finances and your emotions. Necessary expenses for car repairs, buying new appliances, and paying for medical bills may not show up in your three-month expense analysis. You may need to look back over the last year or two to get an idea of what you've spent. Knowing what you've paid out will help you plan ahead.

I understand that it can be challenging to start thinking about saving for car maintenance costs like new tires if you just bought new tires. However, saving now for an expense that you'll incur in two years is wise. Planning ahead will help reduce your stress because you'll have the money when you need it, and you won't have to resort to paying with credit.

Other infrequent expenses to consider getting a handle on are vacations, even if it's just a weekend away. Think about gifts, pet expenses, home goods, and clothes you purchase. How much have you spent on these types of events in the last year or two?

Now think about what you've spent money on that brought you joy? What purchases have given you buyer's remorse? What actions could you have taken before your purchase so that you didn't experience regret? In Chapter 5, I'll teach you how to save like I do for infrequent expenses.

Know Your Numbers

Take the emotional component out of your expenses and see them for what they are: Numbers. If you don't like what you see when you look at your numbers, make adjustments going forward. YOU can direct YOUR money to your needs and wants! Don't let denial, guilt, or fear of being judged interfere with your financial realignment.

When you review your spending patterns, it helps you do three things:

1. When you see your real #s, you gain clarity on where your money is really going.

There is a common tendency to underestimate variable, discretionary expenses. If you were asked how much you spend eating out and you don't really know, you'll probably respond with, "Not that much." When you do the three-month average expenses exercise, you quantify the unknown. "Not that much" may turn into "I spent $2,400 in restaurants over the last three months!"

The same goes for clothes, pets, gifts, vacations, and vehicle maintenance. As you gain clarity around your numbers, be kind to yourself. If what you've spent doesn't derail you from your long-term objectives and you feel no guilt, awesome. Keep living your ideal life! On the other hand, if you experience discomfort by knowing your numbers, that's awesome too. Your discomfort and desire for something better are powerful motivators for transformational change.

2. When you see your real #s, you notice that some of your spending can be shifted to other areas.

When you see that you're spending more on restaurants than you are on savings, investing, or paying off debt, the obvious action is to shift the money from one category to another. Choose to eat out less often. Make a plan to redirect the money you would have spent at restaurants to one of your priority areas. If you're already on track with paying off debt, creating savings, and investing, consider increasing your levels of giving and/or take the vacation you've been denying yourself.

Reallocating your spending, including savings, investing, and giving, is easy when you put systems in place. Systems help you build and protect your wealth so you can have the life$tyle you want! More on systems in Chapter 5.

3. When you see your real #s, you know what it takes to fund your current life$tyle, which allows you to make projections for the future.

Sometimes it's necessary to cut back on spending today to have what you want in the future. However, that's not always the case. If you're on track for your goals and have identified and addressed the unexpected, have some fun with your money. There's a balance you can achieve when you have clarity on your money and values. Tomorrow isn't guaranteed, so don't let your focus on the future become a barrier to enjoying life in the present. Balance your present with your future!

Financial planners love it when you know your #s.

We do love it when you know your life$tyle expenses. Why? Because it's very difficult to give you advice when you're guessing at the details—details we need in order to give you sound guidance. Asking us if you can retire, yet not knowing how much it costs to fund your life$tyle is like playing darts, expecting to hit only bullseyes after being spun around in circles, blindfolded, and having one too many glasses of wine. As my client Wendy Coon, mortgage loan originator at Hometown Lenders, shares, "When you know your numbers, that's when the magic happens!"

Let's design the life you want based on what is true today and what can be true in the future. No more guessing about the present. No more defaulting or "settling" for your days ahead. This is your life and your money. How do you want to live? Who do you want to bless?

Shift and Pivot for Change

Each woman who reads this book is unique, as are her finances and values. You may share similarities in income, expenses, family dynamics, or mindset with another reader; however, you're all unique, just like DNA. What works for one woman may not work for another.

That's why I don't lead with having you create a budget. Instead, I encourage you to start with calculating your net worth because it helps you get organized and gives you one number to know. From that number you can gauge your financial progress.

After that, I have you find out if there are credit issues that need to be dealt with. Those two actions are fairly easy and shouldn't cause overwhelm because it's just some adding, subtracting, and running a few reports. Once you know your net worth and credit, you learn your true numbers. It's more time consuming, but very valuable.

After you've analyzed your life$tyle expenses, the next move is to subtract your expenses from your income over the last three months. You'll see what's right and what's wrong in the way you manage your day-to-day finances.

Income – Expenses = Surplus (or Deficit)

Even though you make great money, you could be spending more than you have coming in, which is the opposite of what you know you should be doing. Reducing or eliminating certain expenses may be in order. If that's a non-negotiable for you, would it make sense to shift some of your free time to an income-producing activity? Only you know the answer to these questions. What are you willing to do to have what you have now? What are you willing to change to have what you want in the long run?

> **BE UNCONVENTIONAL:** Be open to a life pivot, well thought out, of course!

Ladies with a surplus, consider your options for becoming debt-free, building and maintaining your wealth, and being more generous. What is important to you? Why?

Plan Your Spending

Instead of budgeting your entire income and all your expenses, break it all down by your priorities. For example, if vacations are one of your top priorities, have a separate "vacation" account and save throughout the year. Save monthly or per pay period so you have the money to pay for your plane tickets and book your resort. Use this fund to pay for your excursions and incidentals.

If it's hard for you to break away or you don't think you deserve vacations, know that by having funded your vacation account, you have given yourself permission to relax, unwind, and enjoy your downtime. You get to go on vacation, and you aren't bringing any guilt with you!

Tell your money where to go.

Give yourself freedom to spend. I view this as a "macro" approach to personal finance, and I find that it works far better than a "micro" approach. It's an empowering way of looking at your money and all your possibilities.

Budgets, or micro approaches to personal finance, are limiting and seem punitive. No one likes to budget, me included. Know what you want to have money for, then create a **spending plan** and use systems so you have the money you want when you want it, guilt-free! More on this in Chapter 5.

Operating with a spending plan is liberating and allows for flexibility as opposed to rigidity. You can make your money work for you because you're in charge. The more you align your money and values, the more confidence you'll have in the decisions you make.

Debt

If you're debt-free, you can skip this section. If not, stay with me.

Are you carrying any debt? Any debt at all? Even if you only have a mortgage, consider the role debt plays in your life.

- Does your debt feel like a ball and chain?
- Are your payments a burden?
- When you think about the total amount you owe, do you feel mentally drained and overwhelmed?

Did you answer "no" to each of the questions above? Good. I don't want debt to hold you back from your ideal life and that's why I'll pose a "what if" question here. Even though you aren't concerned about your debt, what if you had absolutely no debt payments? What would your life be like? What else could you do with the money that you currently commit to debt repayment?

If you answered "yes" to any of the above questions, that's your signal that you're ready to make changes. You're at the point where a mental shift and financial pivot can change your life. Twenty years ago, I would have answered "yes" to all three of those questions.

After I shifted my mindset and pivoted the way I dealt with my finances, I experienced positive changes in many areas of my life, not just in financial matters. Better career opportunities came my way. I became a mother. My relationships with friends and family improved. My faith in God was renewed. I took action to improve my physical and mental health. I began to give back with my finances and my time. All of these things happened AND I dedicated more time to having fun!

Here are the steps I took to get out of debt. They'll work for you, too!

✓ Analyze your life$tyle

✓ Cut and eliminate expenses

✓ Further your education

✓ Increase your income

✓ List your debt, smallest to largest

✓ Make minimum payments on all debt

✓ Apply all extra income to the debt with the smallest balance

✓ As soon as the debt is paid off, apply that payment toward the next debt

✓ Make payments often—you don't have to wait for the monthly bill

When you're free of debt payments, you'll have more choices and more confidence with your financial situation. You'll have the resources to increase what you give, save, invest, and spend.

Debt-free women are empowered women!

Build Wealth

Your home and your retirement accounts are likely your two largest assets, which makes sense. After all, you need a place to live and the equity in your home usually increases over time. Employer-sponsored retirement plans make it convenient to invest through systematic payroll deductions.

There are other strategies for building wealth, too. Success in those areas depends on many factors. First and foremost, make an agreement with yourself that you'll only invest in things you've taken the time to understand. Haste makes waste.

Take the time to ask questions. Learn the potential trade-offs for upside possibilities and downside risk. How liquid is the investment and what are the tax implications? Are there minimum initial investment requirements? Can you make additions? When and how much? What's the "hassle factor" and do you want the hassle?

You aren't limited to retirement accounts, and you aren't limited to securities. Non-retirement accounts are an option as an alternative, or as a complement to retirement accounts. You can build wealth by investing in one or more businesses, or residential and/or commercial real estate. You can build wealth by saving through bank and credit union accounts or savings bonds. There are many ways to invest and build wealth.

You don't have to feel alone when it comes to figuring out how to build and preserve your wealth, nor do you have to know all the ins and outs. Allow yourself the freedom to be patient and seek wise counsel.

Your wealth team includes your financial planner, accountant, attorney, insurance agent, and mentor or coach. Together, your team will help you address tax treatment, legal matters, access to your money, growth, income, and safety so that you are informed and confident in your decisions.

Financial empowerment gives you:
- ➲ Freedom. You have ready cash for the things you want.
- ➲ Independence (financially and emotionally). You're not someone else's burden.
- ➲ Security. You can create and live the *Lifestyle* you want to live!

GO ROGUE: Personal finance is personal. Figure out what **you** want for **your** freedom, independence, and security. Then plan your plan.

Your money isn't the boss of you unless you let it be.

"Don't Worry About an Emergency Fund," sounds counterintuitive, so let's Go Rogue! with that topic in Chapter 5.

Don't Worry About an Emergency Fund

Abundance is not something we acquire.
It is something we tune into.
—*Wayne Dyer*

Financial celebrities may tell you to have a $1,000 emergency fund while you're paying off debt and, once you're debt free, to keep 3-6 months' worth of expenses available for emergencies. These are rules of thumb that may or may not be ideal for you. Is it any surprise to you at this point in the book that I'm Going Rogue?

Success with money is based on having clarity about what's important to you and the actions you take once you have clear vision. I believe with proper, prior planning, an emergency fund **doesn't** need to be as big as you might think.

If you've been challenged to save money, either for unplanned life events or things you want to have and do in the future, I have solutions for you.

Sinking Funds, Rainy Day Funds, Emergency Funds, Savings Accounts

The concept is the same regardless of what you call them. Setting money aside, over time, for future expenses is a good idea. Or at least, sounds like a good idea, right?

Why is it then that you find it almost impossible to save money? Perhaps you're good at saving money and find it almost impossible to spend money. Why? I'll tell you why: Fear.

Fear can hold you back from living your ideal life. Fear keeps you from having financial resources when emergencies strike and keeps you from optimizing your finances. Fear keeps money on the table.

Fear has you believing your self-imposed, limiting beliefs about your future and about what you can't do to change it. Fear traps you in a cycle of stories you tell yourself, like not being worthy or carrying guilt about financial decisions past, present, and future. Fear keeps your "programming from the past" playing without pause, stop, eject, or erase.

Negative money scripts you may have running on a continuous loop in your head:

I'm fine.

I don't need help with my finances.

I don't have money for that.

I don't have enough money to work with a financial planner.

I could never save up six months of expenses.

Paying cash for a car is impossible.

You can't get an education without taking out student loans.

I have a savings account, but it isn't big enough.

My credit card is my emergency fund.

I don't want to have a whole bunch of accounts to keep track of.

I make good money but can't seem to get ahead.

I'm still trying to get caught up from last year, but I need a vacation.

You know you should have money in savings, whether it's for a rainy day or emergency fund. Why? For protection against financial hardship and the inevitable "unexpected" expenses. What emotions and feelings do you associate with those words? Negative emotions like fear or loss? Maybe guilt or remorse? Financial emergencies can undermine your feeling of security, triggering anxiety and depression. Financial stress can even affect your physical health.

I'm here to help you reframe your mindset about saving and give you an easy-to-implement process so that you have reserves for both expected and unexpected events in your life. And less stress.

"Where's all our money?"

My husband's question, "Where's all our money?" gets my non-snarky response, "It's where it needs to be." Before we were married, my husband kept all his money in one bank account. It made him feel good to look and see a large balance. Even with a large balance, he was challenged to spend money. He was afraid to spend because he didn't have clarity about how much to keep in reserve for upcoming expenses, knowns and unknowns.

Now, nearly ten years into our marriage, he is still befuddled by the very low balance in our checking account. Periodically one of us calls a family finance committee meeting. Whether scheduled or impromptu, we take time to look at our finances. Technology allows us the freedom to hold these discussions wherever we are, provided we have internet. We may hold our finance committee meeting in bed before the start of a long weekend, poolside, dockside, or…[yawn]…in my office.

Finance committee meetings generally start off by looking at our net worth. We compare what it is in the moment to what it was previously, so we can see our progress.

Assets (things you own) – Liabilities (what you owe) = Net Worth

Next, we look at our various account balances and discuss upcoming expenses for projects, purchases, charitable giving, and our ever-important vacation plans!

At this point, I'm excited to be talking finances. I then attempt to show him more of my super cool financial planning reports. At that point? He's done. Checked out. He's satisfied to know our bases are covered, that I'm not running off with the money, and that he can relax and do the things he enjoys like boating and spending time playing with our dog.

Meeting adjourned!

Ladies, if you're like my husband and want to know you're on track for your life$tyle, that your bases are covered, and someone is paying attention to the details so you can spend your time doing the things YOU enjoy doing, create **Sunny Day Funds** to simplify your finances.

Sunny Day Funds (SDFs) in Four Easy Steps
1. Open a checking or savings account and get checks or a debit card
2. Systematically fund the account with automated transfers
3. Use each SDF to pay for its specific expenses
4. Monitor and make periodic adjustments

Some rather famous financial advisors promote the use of envelopes for saving money. Would you feel comfortable keeping several thousand dollars in envelopes? What I propose is that instead of using a paper envelope system, you **use electronic envelopes**.

All you do is systematically fund designated accounts for your upcoming known and unknown expenses. And meet regularly with your financial planner. Having systems in place and regular consultations with your financial team will help you avoid, or at least reduce, your feelings of stress, frustration, and being overwhelmed regarding your finances, because you prepared ahead of time to have money on hand when you need it.

Stay with me. If you think multiple accounts are hard to manage and you're afraid you'll use the wrong account, use a Sharpie to "name" your card. If you're pushing back on setting up multiple accounts for any reason, even though you're inclined to admit they may be an effective way to have money on deck when you need it, realize that you *already* initiated the strategy.

When you started adding to your 401k, you created an account, which you've been systematically funding with the intention to leave it untouched for years—decades really—so that you'd have money available for your life$tyle at the point you decide to stop working.

Like you save systematically for retirement, let's focus on saving money for future expenses. I get it, while at first you may not see the value in having multiple bank accounts, there are benefits. Instead of guessing how much you can afford to spend on various expenses, and instead of guessing or going into debt because you didn't plan ahead, your account balance will tell you how much you can spend.

Think of each of your Sunny Day Funds as a pot of money. You can see how much money is in each pot because each time you log into your online banking account, you'll know at a moment's glance where you stand. My bank's online banking program allows me to put nicknames on my accounts for even greater clarity. I don't have to remember which account is for which expense since the nicknames I've given each account tell how much is available for each category. Pretty cool!

Still concerned about multiple accounts? Account aggregators like WealthVision (LPL Financial), the tool I use with my premium program clients, pulls in all your accounts onto one dashboard. You get a snapshot of your wealth including bank balances, investments, physical assets, debt, and net worth. Plus, you can use it to track and plan your spending. Other tools you can use to track and plan your spending include: Ramsey Solutions, EveryDollar, YNAB (You Need A Budget), and Intuit Mint.

Here are some ideas for your Sunny Day Fund categories:

- Health - insurance premiums, deductible, co-pays, maximum out-of-pocket costs, and prescriptions
- Property taxes
- Transportation - purchase, maintenance, insurance
- Gifts
- Vacation
- Groceries
- Self-care
- Restaurants
- Clothing
- Pets
- College
- Wedding
- Investments - retirement and non-retirement accounts
- Savings – "just because" (for unknowns outside of SDFs)
- Major purchase - business, real estate, dream car, boat, toy, etc.
- Income taxes - quarterly estimates

Using multiple SDF accounts will provide you with the funds to pay cash for purchases instead of resorting to credit. With dedicated accounts, these can help you change your buying patterns because you've evaluated your needs, wants, and impulsivity, so you have control over your money.

You can put into practice SDFs and you'll be glad you did! If you need guidance, just *ask*.

What about Using Credit Cards to Earn Points?

If you choose to use credit cards to earn points, exercise caution. My suggestion is that you don't use credit cards until you have all other debt paid off and you're on track for your saving and investing goals. If that's where you're at, as long as you don't mind spending time managing your card, paying the bill, and managing your points, go for it.

I recommend paying your credit card after each purchase or on a weekly basis. Pay it from the balance in your dedicated SDF. You don't have to wait for the bill to come to pay it. The credit card company wants you to wait for the bill. They count on your missing payments, paying late, and carrying a balance so they make money off you.

Also, when you calculate the value of your points, think about the **value of your time**. How much time did it cost you to manage your points? If you're carrying a credit card balance, it's highly likely that you pay more in interest than you receive in the dollar value of your points. Food for thought. Managing debt takes maturity and discipline. So does saving cash and building up wealth.

Maturity and Discipline

December of 2007 was a significant month for me because it was the first time in 17 years that I didn't finance a car purchase. Up to that point, every car I bought—or, um, leased—came with a payment. It never occurred to me that I could save up and buy a car with cash. Admittedly, I also had champagne taste on a beer budget so I always wanted more car than I could afford. I ended up in a nasty cycle of rolling negative equity into loans and leases.

On top of that, I was also a victim of "going over my miles" on my leases, which was costly. Between 2004 and 2007, I had some realizations, made several new decisions, and acted upon them. When my lease was up, I bought the car out of my lease. Not with cash. I had to finance the car with another loan. At that point, I decided to drive the car into the ground and pay it off ASAP. By the time my little Saturn was using more oil than gas (not literally but close), the loan was paid, and I'd saved enough to pay cash for a used 2007 Jeep Grand Cherokee!

To this day, I pay cash for my vehicles. Instead of buying a brand new car, I let someone else take the hit on depreciation. Each month I systematically make a car payment into my "Vehicle" Sunny Day Fund to have cash ready for the *next* vehicle purchase. Also, I accumulate a balance in my "Vehicle" SDF for the annual insurance bill, maintenance, and repairs.

By the way, even though my husband sells cars, I don't let him "Car Guy" me. I drive what **I** want and he doesn't talk me into financing or leasing. Paying cash is my comfort zone. Why pay a finance company when I can pay myself? Also, I'm not putting myself in a position of carrying the burden of a car note. I'm free!

Many in the car business will attempt to sell you on leasing. No one is going to "sell" me on leasing if they're trying to use the rationale that if I buy new, I won't have to pay for repairs. I've matured and disciplined myself to save for both the vehicle purchase and the repairs in my "Vehicle" SDF. I depend on me.

One other note on vehicles: The discipline of paying cash for my vehicles has changed my behaviors and improved my financial situation. Instead of spending my time always looking at and shopping for cars, I spend my time doing other activities that put money in my pocket, instead of taking it from my pocket. This is the approach that works for me.

You'll need to establish what you're comfortable doing. It may make sense to lease or finance a vehicle while you get your other financial affairs in order. Also, if leasing or financing a vehicle gets you into the vehicle of your dreams and the cost doesn't hold you back from accomplishing your long-term goals, go for it.

My opinion and experience shared here is informational and not biased as to what I believe you should or shouldn't do. Personal finances are personal. My goal is to help you get the results you want in all areas of your life, not just your money! Regardless of your age, your maturity and discipline are your wealth helpers. Setting aside money for a specific purpose and overcoming the temptation to spend, takes maturity and discipline.

Sunny Day Funds reduce your need for a big rainy day fund.

It Really Works!

The Sunny Day Fund strategy has worked for me and my clients.

Prior to utilizing my SDF system, Sheri was burdened with debt and stressed as she tried to figure out how to move money around to pay bills on time. We

67

analyzed her cash flow, income, and expenses, which included how she spent her "fun" money.

One of the first steps she took was to pay off debt. Gone now are the mortgage and credit card debt. Without debt payments, she has freed up extra money every month. After paying off the debt, she implemented a combination of paper and electronic envelopes, based on the types and frequency of her purchases. Today, confident and empowered with her money for the first time in her 60+ years, Sheri has more money in the bank than she's ever had in her life. She'll tell you, **"I feel so good now!"**

Another client began the process of tracking her expenses like we discussed in Chapter 4, and discovered that her dog was getting a bigger allowance than she was! Because Rachel had clarity about her current and future finances, she had the confidence to increase her "Self-Care" SDF without jeopardizing her long-term financial goals. For you, maybe it's Botox, manicures, or massages that are included in your self-care fund. We'll talk more about giving yourself permission for some luxury splurges in Chapter 11.

Save Time with SDFs

Unless you keep a spreadsheet or some type of ledger, a single savings account doesn't clearly show you what's available today for a particular expense. There's a high probability you'll underestimate or overestimate what you actually have available to spend.

There's also the matter of timing. Not having clarity about how much you'll need and when you'll need it, produces challenges. Speaking of time management, tracking on a spreadsheet or with a ledger requires an allocation of your schedule. I know you'd like to have more time in your day, not less, so let's put some minutes/hours back into your day by considering automated transfers into your SDFs. Easy to set up and manage!

Create and Manage Your Own "Escrow" Account

Are you afraid to pay off your mortgage because you won't have an escrow account to rely on for your property taxes and insurance? Create and manage your own escrow account as another Sunny Day Fund. Once you know your numbers and are set up for systematic transfers, all you do is pay the insurance bill or property tax bill before it's due.

Sunny Day Fund (SDF)

Needs
(how much you need)

÷

Months
(how long you have)

=

Monthly Amount to Fund
(what you need per month)

Set up a "Home" SDF (or possibly labeled with part of the property address such as "1824" or "Maple Lane" or "1824 Maple Lane"). Here's a sample chart for calculating how much is needed to fund this type of savings plan for homeowners over time:

Annual property taxes	$12,000
($8,000 summer and $4,000 winter)	
Annual insurance	$ 2,000
Maintenance/Repairs/Improvements	$ 1,200
Insurance deductible	$ 1,200
Appliance replacement	$ 1,200
	$17,600

Optional savings plans to achieve $17,600 in a year:
$1,466 per month

$ 733 per pay period, twice monthly

$ 677 per pay period, every other week

$ 338 per week

Keep in mind that if your property taxes are due in the near future, depending on a 12-month savings schedule likely won't work for you. Shorten it to the number of available months prior to the due date.

Let's say toward the end of April you decide to start saving cash for your September property tax bill. First of all, good job for planning ahead! You'll want to determine how much is due. For example, if your $8,000 property tax bill is due on September 15, divide by the number of pay periods between now and the due date. If you have two pay periods each month for May, June, July, and August and one in September, that's nine pay periods. Divide $8,000 by 9 = $889.

Now set up an $889 deposit per pay period as a systematic transfer into your Home SDF for your property taxes. After the bill is paid, adjust the transfer to an amount equal to one-twelfth ($\frac{1}{12}$) of your total annual property taxes. In this scenario, you can thereby reduce the systematic transfer for property taxes to $500/pay period. That's a savings of nearly $400 per pay period! What could you do with that extra $400?

My advice is to redirect the savings of $400 per pay period to another one of your priorities!

This strategy of planning ahead for future expenses, using **systems** to save for the future, and making adjustments over time will save you a lot of time. You'll also minimize the headaches that come from forgetting to make a manual transfer. If this seems overwhelming or you simply don't have time or the desire to figure it all out, a financial coach can help.

Vacation Sunny Day Fund

For those of you who love to travel but sometimes feel guilty that you're spending too much on vacations, open an account specifically for vacations. The money you accumulate in this SDF is your permission slip. It's your passport for your vacation and because you have permission, you don't need to feel guilty.

For those of you who want to take your entire family on a special vacation, I offer the same suggestion. Open an account specifically for vacations. If you find it challenging to save, open an account at a different bank than you normally use and don't get online access to your new getaway account. This will help keep you from the temptation of moving money around. Set up a systematic transfer from your main bank account to your vacation account at the other bank. You can do this either through your online banking service as bill pay, a transfer via a program like Zelle, or ask your banker to set it up for you.

Figure out your trip's budget and when you want to go. For example, if you want to go on a trip three years from now that will cost you $10,000, save $278 per month for 36 months. The money will be there for your memory-making adventure!

This concept is an easy-to-implement system that can work for you. Just remember **why** it's so important that you take this vacation or take multiple vacations. The concept of "why" is important. Your why will help you stay focused on your values and priorities.

For many retirees, the first five years of retirement are years when spending goes up dramatically because every day becomes a Saturday. What do you do on Saturday? Chores? Where do you go? Grocery shopping. Home Depot. You're going to the places and doing the things you've wanted to do but put off all week. **Projects and hobbies take time and cost money.**

I endorse proper, prior planning for the things that are important to you like your home. And that includes having money set aside for repairs, taxes, and insurance.

Take a walk through your home and property. Look at your furnace—how old is it? How much life does it still have left? What would it cost to replace it if you had to today? Make a list as you go through your home: Water heater, water softener, air conditioner, washer, dryer, stove, dishwasher, and refrigerator. They won't all need to be replaced at the same time, but what if the two most expensive ones did? Set that much aside now in an SDF for these expenses.

If one key appliance goes out, you'll have an emergency on your hands. Wouldn't it be great to have money saved up specifically for that expense, so you don't need to dip into your Vacation SDF?

Just-Because Fund

When you create and fund your Sunny Day Funds, it reduces your need for a big emergency fund. I suggest having a Just-Because Fund for the one-off expenses that don't fall into your other SDF categories. This could include losing your job or a situation where you make a well-thought-out decision to help someone financially.

How much to keep in your Just-Because Fund is up to you. There is nothing wrong with using the 3-6 months' worth of expenses (or income) rule of thumb. Are you on track for all your other financial and life$tyle goals, including funding your SDFs? How secure are your sources of income? What does your intuition tell you about the right amount? Go with your gut-instinct. Whatever number comes to mind is probably fine, especially if you've eliminated debt, are saving and investing for the future, and have the quality of life you desire.

Your Just-Because Fund can be cash, a bank account, or an investment account. I've found that men want very little in liquid savings and tend to move it all

FROM

TO

Savings

(SDF)
(Sunny Day Fund)

Emergency Fund

Just Because Fund

to their investments. They don't like the idea of missing out on the returns they could get in the market. Many women, however, tend to be more cautious in the sense of balancing safety, liquidity, and growth of their money.

While you can build up a cash balance inside a non-retirement investment account, be prepared for taxes due to gains when you sell investments in the account. It's important to balance cash-type savings with investments so that you have flexibility when it comes to taxes. Sometimes it makes sense to sell an investment, especially if you can take a tax loss or have become too heavily concentrated in a particular sector. Before selling any investment, consult with your financial planner and accountant!

You'll be glad to know that in non-IRA accounts, you won't have the 10% IRS penalty that comes with premature withdrawals from retirement accounts. Also, very important, most investments are subject to market fluctuations. You can lose money. In the event of a *just-because situation*, do you want to withdraw from your account if it's worth less than what you originally invested? Would you have wished you had deposited the Just-Because money in a bank account?

I'm not suggesting that you shouldn't invest in securities or other types of investments that go up and down in value. What I am recommending is that you're wise to have a sound financial foundation in place, which includes having a plan for future expected and unexpected expenses, before making any kind of investment. Bottom line: The more income you have and the higher your net worth, the more choices you have. And perhaps fewer frustrations.

Many of the women I surveyed for this book shared with me that high on their list of priorities was making sure they were in a financial position to assist if their children needed help. In my opinion, your adult children's emergencies aren't your emergencies. You have no moral obligation to ante up. However, if your finances are in order and if giving of your financial resources doesn't shortchange your own financial security and ability to maintain your life$tyle, go ahead. Be a blessing and help!

At a minimum, if you don't implement the Sunny Day Funds system and are curious about the least amount you need in savings, I suggest you look at your health insurance out-of-pocket (OOP) maximum and the deductible on both your home and auto insurance policies. Now that you know these numbers, add them up. The total is your answer.

74

BE UNCONVENTIONAL: When an expense arises, whether expected or not, express gratitude that you had the money to pay for it and that you're actually helping others by paying your bill or making the purchase. It's not just about the cost to you, it's also about the benefit to others.

Bite-Size Pieces

My friend who decided to quit smoking, quit drinking, start working out, and go on a keto diet, realized that doing too many new things at one time was a recipe for failure. Same with your finances. Start incrementally to organize and implement your Sunny Day Funds.

To avoid the feeling of overwhelm, open just one new bank account per month until you have all your SDFs covered. Remember to plan for both expected and unexpected future expenses. After you open an account, set up a systematic transfer to build up your SDF balance. The timing of your systematic transfer is up to you. Some of my clients make monthly transfers, others by pay period, and others quarterly or annually.

Implementing and using your SDF system won't be perfect, especially at first. Monitor and adjust until you find what works for you! Side note: Name a beneficiary(ies) when you open SDFs just in case something happens to you. Naming beneficiaries is an act of love and will simplify things for your loved ones.

Here's a quick recap:
- ✓ Approach your finances by starting with your values and knowing why you're motivated to try new approaches to your cash management practices.
- ✓ Instead of your money being in one big savings account, SDFs are dedicated to specific expenses.
- ✓ The nickname you place on each account, each pot of money, tells you where you stand at a moment's glance.
- ✓ Systematic transfers to fund your SDFs saves time.

Knowing your why will help you say "no" to the actions that don't serve you today or down the road. Get someone to hold you accountable. Your friends and family probably won't be up for the task because they love you and don't want to put you in an uncomfortable situation. They may even go so far as to help you rationalize your choices with potentially poor outcomes. There is value in hiring a professional to keep you accountable to your goals.

What if...?

I like to ask myself, "What if…" when I'm navigating both difficult and positive situations. What if I could pay cash for a car? What if I could go on a vacation and not have those bills hang over me when I get my credit card bill?

What is it that you REALLY want in life that you don't already have?

_____

_____

_____

_____

Why is it important to you to have that thing(s)?

_____

_____

What is the best possible outcome if you pursue this goal?

_____

_____

How can you accomplish your goals?

_____

_____

Would an SDF help?

_____

_____

SDFs work when you do the front-end work of opening accounts, determining how much should be contributed to the accounts, and having the systematic transfers in place. Look back at your spending over the last few months (or year) and use your averages to come up with the amounts for your systematic transfers. On the back end, pay for expenses from the dedicated account.

Your Sunny Day Funds are your system for success. They help reduce financial risks and associated stresses and frustrations. You'll need to define and refine the details for your SDFs, so ask for help and get advice from qualified people to help you get on the fast track for your ideal life$tyle.

If you're ready to embrace an abundance mindset, ditch scarcity habits, and move to a space of gratitude, it's your time for SDFs!

GO ROGUE: Out of sight, out of mind. Get money out of your main account and into dedicated accounts so you don't overspend, and you're prepared when you need to be. It works!

In Chapter 4, I advised you to not start with creating a budget. In this chapter, I gave you advice on how and why Sunny Day Funds reduce your need for savings for a big rainy day fund. A word of caution: Beware of advice from people who are broke, who don't understand opportunity cost, or who are burdened with negativity surrounding money.

More in Chapter 6, "Don't Take this Advice"...

Don't Take This Advice

The gullible believe anything they're told;
the prudent sift and weigh every word.
Proverbs 14:15 (MSG)

If you're in the position of bestowing advice, this chapter will help you avoid mistakes you could be making when you're actually trying to be helpful. If you're on the receiving end of advice, this chapter may not be as exciting as you'd like. Stay with me, though, because the lessons you'll learn on this slower path are invaluable and can fast-track you to thriving in your own optimized life. Hey, I didn't promise conventional wisdom...I'm Going Rogue!

Lessons Learned

Real Estate

You've heard it said, "For what you'd pay in rent, you could own a home and be building equity." My lesson learned in hindsight with my first home purchase was that the conventional wisdom "owning is better than renting" didn't apply to me at the time.

CAVEAT EMPTOR

Let the buyer beware.

In theory, the advice to buy rather than rent wasn't bad, it's just that the advice wasn't the best advice considering my situation. The problem was that relevant factors, including my finances and behaviors, weren't taken into consideration.

When you hear, "You should…" listen, then exercise your ability to use discernment. Had I used sound judgment, thought ahead, and sought expert advice—specifically how to consider the pros and cons of home ownership—I'd have saved thousands of dollars.

When I decided that I'd buy my first home, I had zero in savings and used my tax refund for the down payment. The only "knowledge" I had about the financial implications of owning a home was that I'd be building equity. Interest rates, down payment, and PMI (Private Mortgage Insurance) weren't anything I considered. All I knew, or thought I knew, was that my payment was less than I'd pay in rent, and that if I rented, I wouldn't have an asset to sell later.

I had no concept of the **cost of home ownership**. Decorating, maintenance, improvements, and appliances all cost money. The credit card companies loved me because credit is how I paid for my expenses while owning a home. My first house was a "fixer-upper." My dad made many structural improvements for me, but my house needed more and more. After five years, I sold it at a loss. Plus, I'd accumulated thousands in credit card debt, much of it attributed to the home, because I didn't have a good foundation in personal finance.

Now that I do have solid financial footing, I'm able to use my experience to help you avoid the mistakes I made!

Credit

My first home taught me lessons about thinking ahead and having a plan. I learned that it's easy to go into debt, and it's much harder to get out of debt. Building credit wasn't something I had to do to buy my first home. I'd been building my credit for almost a decade at that point.

At age 18, I opened my first credit card. Having been told "we can't afford it" nearly all my life, credit was my ticket to having GUESS® jeans, Polo Ralph Lauren® Oxfords, and Coach® handbags. Ignoring my mom's advice about making sure I had enough money to pay my bills in full every month, I built my credit and accumulated a huge amount of debt that didn't get paid off until I was in my 30s.

If you're just starting out or if you're in reset mode with your finances, resist the advice you hear about building your credit by getting a credit card or loan in your name. Instead, **build a strong financial foundation first**.

Exercise behaviors that will serve you for a lifetime. Check off where you are so far:

_____ Chapter 1 - Remind yourself what you want to accomplish in life.

_____ Chapter 2 - Invest in yourself.

_____ Chapter 3 - Embrace generosity and abundance.

_____ Chapter 4 - Know your numbers.

_____ Chapter 5 - Use Sunny Day Funds to be prepared for known and unknown expenses.

If you're struggling with debt and poor credit, you won't find your solution by going deeper into debt. Stop using credit, buy only what you need, pay cash, and pay your debt payments on time, every time.

Retirement

Conventional advice about investing for retirement is that you should start as soon as possible. You'll get the benefit of compounding returns over time, which potentially reduces the amount you'll need to invest over time and if your employer offers a matching contribution, you get "free" money. I agree with that advice to start investing as soon as possible, as long as you have your ducks in a row! If you're on track, start investing. If you're not, delay investing for retirement.

You can segment these types of accounts and decide to invest or save based on your timeline.

- **Short-term expenses:** Readiness for emergencies and life$tyle purchases within the next 3 years.

- **Intermediate-term expenses:** Purchases generally planning to make 3-7 years from now. For example, replacing your vehicle or buying a home.

- **Long-term expenses:** Typically more than 7 years in the future, could include retirement, weddings, college tuition, a second home, investment real estate, etc.

The more time you have before you'll need access to some or all of the money, the more aggressive you can be with your investments. The less time you have, the more conservative your investment approach should be.

To make sure you have the money when you need it and that you haven't lost value due to market fluctuations, I recommend that for emergencies and purchases you'll make in less than three years, that you don't invest. Instead, use bank accounts like checking, savings, CDs, and money market accounts to build and preserve your money because with these types of accounts, your money isn't subject to the ups and downs that can happen in investment accounts.

Being conservative and not investing for the short term could mean giving up potential gains that exceed what you'd earn in bank accounts. That's okay in my opinion. You're foregoing potential returns in exchange for the stability and confidence that the money is there when you need it.

Jumping into long-term retirement investing can cost you big time if you haven't arranged for the short and intermediate terms. Let's say something comes up in the short term and you have nothing saved except in your retirement accounts. You could use credit and pay potentially high interest rates or you might withdraw from an IRA. Withdrawals from traditional IRAs before age 59½ come with a 10% penalty plus ordinary income tax.

You might be able to take a loan from your 401k, but not all plans allow loans. The trouble with 401k loans is if you leave your employer and can't pay the loan back in full, you're taxed and penalized on the unpaid balance. Like withdrawals from traditional IRAs, you are subject to ordinary income tax plus a 10% penalty. Not only do you take the tax hit, but now there's less, maybe even $0 dedicated to retirement, which means you'll be further behind on your retirement goals.

Plan ahead for the short term to avoid sabotaging your long-term goals.

- ⊃ Ask for guidance about the types of accounts that are appropriate based on your intended use and time frame.
- ⊃ Always seek the advice of a tax professional and your investment professional before taking premature withdrawals from retirement accounts.

Taxes

Advice commonly given on the topic of taxes is to take actions like the following. Do any of these sound familiar?

"Invest in your retirement account for the tax deduction."

What about alternative ways of thinking? What about paying the tax now and letting your account grow 100% tax free?

"Get the deduction now while you're working; you'll be in a lower tax bracket when you're retired."

Really? You could find yourself in a higher income tax bracket when you retire because you built wealth. Also, what if the IRS tax brackets change and go up?

"Make a charitable donation so you get the tax deduction."

By now, you know that I believe in generosity and giving time and money. Give for the right reasons and if there's a side benefit, such as a tax advantage in the gift, by all means, utilize it. You may need to drastically up your giving plan in order to actually get the tax benefit. Review your tax returns with your accountant and financial planner and have a discussion about your charitable giving goals. Together, they can help you plan the most effective strategies for tax-advantaged giving.

"Why pay off your mortgage when you can get a tax deduction?"

This question, cloaked as advice, is a good question. It assumes that by carrying a mortgage, you in fact are getting a tax deduction, which may not be the case given the historically low mortgage interest rate environment, the standard deduction, and your tax bracket. Looking at the numbers is the **quantitative** side of the discussion.

There's also the **qualitative** side of the equation to factor into your decision. Take for example, Jessica. She's single, 100% debt-free, has her "ducks in a row," and made the decision to purchase her house with cash.

She considered both her finances and heart. Jessica felt more secure by not having the weight of a mortgage. She is free to make decisions on how to spend her money, like on vacations, without the nagging sense of having made the wrong decision in getting a mortgage. Now, instead of paying the bank for the next 15 years, she's paying herself by investing what would have been her mortgage payment.

If she earns an average of 7% per year over the next 15 years on this investment, she'll potentially have accumulated over $560,000. And…with a paid-for house the entire time!

"Why would you ever pay off your house? You can make more money in the market."

Like Jessica, I'm glad that my house was paid off before I quit a high-income job to start my own business. Building a business from the ground up was stressful and it would have been even more so if I'd been burdened with a house payment. I'll agree, there are opportunities to make more in the market than you'd pay in interest. However, I'd rather have the security of being 100% the homeowner and not sharing "ownership" with the bank.

Another woman, Wendy, has no regrets about paying her mortgage off early. After she sold one of her investment properties, she told me she wanted to buy a new truck, go on a cruise, and have enough for capital gains taxes.

Being highly coachable, she took my advice. Instead of buying a new vehicle, I suggested she pay off her mortgage and start saving for future purchases using the Sunny Day Fund strategy. She'll tell you that instead of feeling financially stressed, she feels blessed to have a home that was paid for in full when she couldn't work due to the COVID-19 shutdown.

Investing

Here's what I've learned about "hot investments". When *everyone* is talking about a particular way to make a killing, exercise caution. Before investing for retirement or in a non-retirement account, it's best to have your financial house in order. See Chapters 1-5.

Direct Sales

Can you make money in direct sales? Yes. However, most people don't. Research, research, research. Will you be selling a product, business opportunity, or both? Do you love sales? Do you have the time to build a business? Do you have the will to do whatever it takes to make it big in network marketing? Look for any red flags and ask questions. "No thank you," is powerful.

If you love learning, direct sales could be more of an opportunity for self-improvement than an immediate income source. I know of individuals who will say that their experience in direct sales was life changing. The education, motivation, and leadership skills they developed were building blocks to success in future endeavors.

Pampered Chef® changed my life. I loved the products and still love them to this day. It was the business opportunity that changed everything for me. Here's the twist: I was in Pampered Chef® for the relatively quick money that came from selling their products, which I was using to help get out of debt. However, a woman decided she'd like to become a consultant and during the time I spent onboarding her, she "up-boarded" me to what has become my life's purpose in helping women get what they want in life. She passed my resume on to her boss, who passed it to a competitor, who ended up hiring me. My experience with direct sales changed the course of my life.

Sorting Out Advice

Google, social media, and day-to-day conversations are sources of free advice especially when it comes to smart money moves you could be making. What you should do though, isn't for anyone to say. You have the freedom to make choices, so choose wisely. Before taking action, consider the advice you've been given and its relevance for your situation. Empower yourself to delay instant gratification so that you can seek wise counsel. Ask about potential problems to consider, to understand the challenges and pitfalls of taking advice on credit, home ownership, and retirement accounts.

My advice, it's *really* good advice: Become a life-long-learner. Education is an investment in yourself—refer back to Chapter 2 for a refresher. If you take action with your education, it leads to transformation. You're already investing in yourself by reading this book. My advice on what to do next when it comes to your finances, is **get professional advice**. There are financial professionals who will coach, teach, and mentor you, even if you don't have much to invest. You may pay for the advice, but think of it as an investment. Not asking for advice can often be more expensive.

Acting on well-intentioned advice can cost you. Big time!

When you ask for counsel, make sure you've given an accurate and complete picture of both your finances and your behavioral tendencies. Without the full picture, any advice you act upon could be costly. Also, ask good questions. One of my favorites is, "What else should I be asking?"

BE UNCONVENTIONAL: Your financial success is defined by YOU and you alone. Financial success is a marathon, not a sprint. Take it slow. Be comfortable with YOUR decision to build a strong foundation. Otherwise, failing to do so can cost you time and money as you try to clean up financial messes.

Where to Start

⮑ Start thinking about the long-term outcomes of decisions you make today.

⮑ Don't follow the crowd.

⮑ Stop searching for quick fixes to years of problems.

⮑ Do seek wise counsel.

⮑ Go confidently with your decisions after doing your due diligence.

GO ROGUE: Often, I've found that I've learned my biggest lessons not in the moment, but during times of introspection and reflection. Give yourself 10-15 minutes in a quiet place to go down memory lane and consider the lessons you've learned in hindsight. Use the space below to journal what you've learned and how your lessons could benefit someone else.

_____

_____

_____

_____

_____

My wish for you is that you have everything you want in life. Take into consideration the advice that comes your way. **Reflect on how advice, even well-intentioned advice, applies to you now and how your decisions today could impact you in the future.** It's okay to Go Rogue! and take unconventional paths to wealth. The key to the wealth you desire is taking action and heeding the lessons learned along the way.

Next in Chapter 7, "Don't Wait for Wealth," I'm sharing practical, start-right-here-right-now concepts to help you live YOUR ideal life.

Don't Wait for Wealth

It takes as much energy to wish as it does to plan.
—Eleanor Roosevelt

I'm Going Rogue! Luck has little to nothing to do with building and keeping wealth.

Proactive Wealth

So many of you have told me that the most important thing about money is security. You find security in being able to afford the things you need and want, by being able to help others, and knowing you have money for the future.

What is it, then, that keeps you from getting professional advice so that you can experience confidence and peace with your finances? Hope and faith for a better future is a good way to approach money. But you can make your situation even better by doing something about it! Are your mindset and behaviors saboteurs of your wealth? Even with an abundance attitude, if you wish for luck with money, yet do nothing to build wealth, your inaction delays you from having what you really want: **Wealth for a great quality of life**.

> **BE UNCONVENTIONAL:** With the right mindset and systems, building and keeping wealth can be easy.

Easy? Yes—When You Embrace the Process!

- ➲ Take action.
- ➲ Start asking for help so you can build and keep your wealth.
- ➲ Don't accept your own negative self-talk.
- ➲ Stop waiting for money to make you feel better.
- ➲ Do a self-check on your value systems. Inspect what you expect of yourself and your team.
- ➲ Go ahead and get involved with your wealth.

Proper, Prior Preparation

Every experience in life is preparation for the future. That's why I believe having a solid financial foundation prepares you for success in life. As you save and invest, you're saying "no" to something in the moment in order to be able to say "yes" to unknown opportunities in the future.

Athletes are a great example of individuals who are always preparing ahead of time, even in their off seasons. Training is necessary all year long, not just while "in season." Preparing for excellence requires a comprehensive approach for optimal results: Mental toughness, proper nutrition, and overall fitness. Athletes engage in a variety of physical fitness training, cardio, strength, and flexibility, so they can perform at peak levels.

Like athletes, *training* **for wealth all the time is essential for lasting results**. If you want to build and preserve your wealth, you'll always be in training. The good news is that systems and your team of financial trainers will help make it easier and less time-consuming than trying to do everything all on your own.

Doing it on your own could turn into a full-time job and keep you from spending time with the people who mean the most to you. Trying to DIY (Do It Yourself) every facet of your finances comes at a cost of your time, money, or both. You don't know what you don't know until it's too late. If personal finance isn't your passion, delegate so you can focus on what gives you joy and what matters to you. Delegating helps you live your ideal life. It doesn't mean you get to ignore your wealth, rather it frees you up to **oversee** rather than do all the work.

An Unpleasant Surprise

When he walked into the living room, she immediately knew something was wrong. He'd just come from his office where multiple monitors were lit up in flashing rainbow colors. At home, they split up the financial responsibilities. She handled the day-to-day finances while he handled the investments. He'd been trading for years and had built a mid-six-figure portfolio.

The look he had that day was because their wealth had practically evaporated overnight. All but a few thousand dollars was lost when the market moved faster than he could sell out. It's a true story of a DIY investor who didn't want to pay for portfolio management, who wasn't diversifying, and didn't have safeguards in

place for investments that were highly concentrated in a single sector.

Fortunately for their love and commitment to each other, the marriage survived and they're slowly rebuilding what was lost.

Build

For wealth that lasts, **you don't have to wait for a windfall**. You can accumulate your own wealth. Part One was Your Vision, Your Reality: Live your Ideal Life. If you understand your motivation for building wealth, you'll stay focused.

- ⮑ When you invest in yourself, you're spending time and money to prepare *yourself* for the future.
- ⮑ When you save and invest money, you're preparing your *finances* for the future.
- ⮑ Giving of your resources is an investment in *someone else's* future.

Investing in yourself and engaging in acts of generosity, may seem like conflicting ideas, but they're actually similar. The common thread is that the choices you make indicate that you have confidence in your decisions to save and give. In the present and in the future. Clarity on how much to invest and give will help ease feelings of fear, guilt, and scarcity. Gain clarity by working with a financial planner who'll help you see what it takes to support your life$tyle.

Wealth is no accident.
Building wealth is not an accident and neither is keeping wealth.
Both situations require patience, maturity, guidance,
and clarity on your values and financial situation.

Rome wasn't built in a day and your net worth won't be either. However, over time you can build wealth by being disciplined and mature. You can set up systems to save time and make your money go where you want it to go. Your financial team can help you build wealth if you let them, and if you follow their advice.

When you've prepared yourself for wealth, it will be easier to keep it and make it grow. Your strong financial foundation prepares you to make investments in things that can make money for you. This could be investing in securities, but it isn't limited to market-related investments. Perhaps you enjoy and see value in collectibles, antiques, or other types of property. Do you have the cash on hand to make a purchase that could net you big profits?

Are your behaviors with money strong enough to keep it? If you received an unexpected influx of money, would you have anything to show for it in five years? Be prepared to keep your money. What about keeping money you receive when you sell an investment? Are your behaviors such that you'd be able to have some fun with the proceeds, as well as set some aside for a future investment?

Your wealth is your security and it's also there for your use. You can use your money for investing and growing your net worth, enhancing your life$tyle, and giving. Ideally, you use your wealth for a combination of all three.

Protect

Diversification, or keeping your eggs in **multiple baskets**, is a strategy that doesn't give you any guarantees. With diversification, you aren't promised anything, but it can help reduce the impact of a financial loss and provide opportunities for increased returns.

Have you heard a business owner say they don't invest for retirement? That their business is their "retirement"? Investing solely in your business is a big financial risk. It's the same thing as betting all your money on only one stock or in a single sector of the market. It can be a huge gamble; a gamble I bet you aren't willing to take. While the thrill of quick gains can be alluring and keep you coming back for more, remember that as quick as you can make money by betting, the returns can be taken from you just as fast. Diversify!

Invest in things you understand and with an amount that wouldn't devastate your finances in the event of partial or complete loss. Remember Enron and WorldCom? Two examples of what not to do. Employees saw a huge opportunity to make money by buying their company stock; some invested 100% of their retirement account in their own company stock. Those who did, lost virtually everything when fraud and corruption were revealed.

What I've noticed over the last 20 years, is that if everyone is talking about a particular investment, there may be a bubble coming. The late 90s rush to invest in tech left investors reeling after that bubble burst in the early 2000s. Later, there were rising real estate values before the corresponding housing crisis.

What's next? Crypto currency? As you invest in trends, get professional advice so that you understand what's at risk, how to potentially reduce your risk with a diversified portfolio, and how much is suitable to invest based on your financial situation.

Transfer Risk

Professional advice is especially important when you want to protect the wealth you've already built, especially if you were to have a health crisis and became unable to work anymore. During your working years, **disability insurance** will help provide an income if that were to happen. Statistics show that your probability of becoming disabled during your working years is higher than the probability of your dying. Most individuals will insure their lives to leave money for those left behind, while failing to insure their income for their own lifetime.

Gina didn't know what she didn't know. Each year during Open Enrollment for employee benefits she'd look through the list of available coverage, make her selections, and not think about it again until the following year. You see, when Gina and I started her initial financial plan, I noticed that while she had short-term disability insurance, she didn't have long-term disability coverage.

She didn't actually need short-term disability because Gina had well over six months' worth of income in savings at the bank plus non-retirement investments. However, if she were to have become disabled without having **long-term disability** coverage, based on her age and income at the time of disability, it could have cost her millions of dollars in lost wages.

The following enrollment period we met, reviewed all of the employee benefits, and she added long-term disability insurance. Gina shared with me, "Your fees are more than worth it to help me avoid a potential mistake like that."

The other life event that most take a gamble on is the cost associated with becoming frail. No one wants the nursing home to take their money, right? Are they "taking" your money or are you paying for a service? According to the Genworth Financial Cost of Care Survey 2020, the national average cost for **long-term care** in a semi-private room was over $93,000 per year. There are alternatives to consider, including the location and cost of care. Proper, prior planning will help put you at ease and make it much less difficult for those making care decisions on your behalf.

Past performance is not indicative of future results. This is good to know when you make investments that can go up and down in value. When you make an investment in a market-related security, I can't give you any guarantees as to how much you'll make in the short run or the long run. One of the guarantees I can give you is that at some point in your life, you're going to die. No one gets out of here alive, so it's a good idea to have your affairs in order. If others are relying on you to provide for them financially, you can **use life insurance** to offer financial protection in the event that you unexpectedly pass away.

A strategy I like to use with my clients who are executing large **Roth IRA conversions** is to use a life insurance policy to "make up" the initial tax hit. As a general example, a single woman with a $1,000,000 traditional IRA who wants to convert it in full to a Roth IRA could give up $400,000 to Uncle Sam. With time in the market, the $600,000 that's left after taxes, will grow tax-free but it will take time. While waiting, she has peace knowing her beneficiaries would get the Roth IRA account plus the proceeds from her life insurance policy if she were to pass before the market recouped what she paid out in taxes. If you're contemplating a Roth conversion, this isn't a firm recommendation, but rather a strategy to be explored considering the other variables in your financial picture.

wind·fall
'win(d)fôl
a piece of unexpected good fortune, typically one
that involves receiving a large amount of money.

What's considered a **windfall** differs from woman to woman. An unexpected amount of money that comes your way might not be significant to you, but for another, that same amount could be life changing. Either way, it's important to have good habits and boundaries, an abundance mindset for all the possibilities that lay ahead for you, and a solid financial foundation so that you make wise financial choices when money you didn't earn comes your way.

If you're in the financial position where a windfall wouldn't change your life, I encourage you to consider what you would do with the money. Would you put it in the bank or invest it? Would you give some or all of it away? When? Would you include planned giving as a component of your estate plan? What about establishing a scholarship fund or foundation? All of the above?

Don't Wait for Your Knight in Shining Armor

There's a cost to being rescued if you didn't learn from it. Unfortunately, the lessons embedded in the rescue tend to be those discovered in hindsight. Exercise foresight and look out for "red flags." Understand the tradeoffs. If you allow yourself to be rescued, it could turn out to be a dream come true (I know there are good situations) or, we all know there are some nightmare situations too.

I hope you haven't lived this nightmare. One "knight" dated women who didn't make much money. He'd shower them with gifts, jewelry, clothes, cars, and implants. He'd get them to quit their jobs and stay at home, taking away their ability to earn and manage their own money. Work took him on the road where it would get lonely. Alcohol, drugs, and women filled the gaps and emptied his bank accounts. The pattern was the same every time. Eventually, the stay-at-home girlfriend would decide it was time to start over from scratch. In addition to finding a new home, she had to find work and begin the process of rebuilding her confidence and finances.

A confident and financially independent woman is attractive. She can take care of herself and doesn't depend on a man for money. I want to help you build and protect your wealth for the stability, relationships, and fun you desire in life.

Building and keeping wealth is a rewarding discipline that results in confidence and empowerment!

If You Find Yourself a Party of One

In the days after her husband's unexpected death, struggling with the emotions she was experiencing, her grief turned to anger. She was great at making money, but at home, the bills and investments were his responsibility. There was a time when they looked at their finances together. Reviewing the numbers gave her confidence that all was well and that they were on the right financial track for their future. A substantial seven-figure net worth was projected at retirement.

At some point in their marriage, she stopped being intentional about looking at their finances and just let him handle the money. She stopped inspecting what she expected. You can understand her anger when in the midst of handling his affairs, she discovered that he had stopped paying their life insurance premiums, drained their savings and investments, and accumulated huge amounts of debt.

The only thing that saved her after this crisis was her confidence. She knew she could survive, rebuild emotionally, and reestablish her own financial security. Intentional became Carri's middle name!

While coming to terms with the idea that your money and your future is your sole responsibility, which can seem like a lot to handle, I have good news for you: You don't have to *default* into your future. And you don't have to figure out your finances alone!

You can surround yourself with supportive, like-minded people who'll be there for you. Beyond supportive friends and family, you can form a team of professionals to help guide you in areas outside your comfort zone, like taxes, insurance, investing, and planning.

Typically, women come to me wondering if they're on the right track, if they're making mistakes, and want to know what else they should be doing. Or, a woman knows she should be doing something, but doesn't know exactly how or where to start. Don't wait to find out if you're on target with your finances to **think about your dreams**. I encourage you to start dreaming and exploring the question, "What if…?" now.

The wealth you possess is a tool to serve others, to be a blessing.

If you've let go of your dreams, quashed your vision of what you really want, or keep yourself from even thinking about possibilities, it's time to Go Rogue! You have choices and you can do anything you set your mind to. You have the freedom to choose where you live, where you work, the income you make, how you spend your free time and with whom.

When you work with me, it's about the entire picture and bridging the gap between what you've got and what you really want. Wealth Management is more than managing investments; what I do is help you manage your quality of life.

"What do you *really* want?"
- What brings you joy?
- What fulfills you?
- What do you look forward to doing?
- Who do you love spending time with?

⊃ If money were no object, what would you spend your time doing and who would you do it with?

⊃ What could make your quality of life even better?

Don't Expect a 30-Second Solution to a 30-Year Problem

My job is to help you align your money with the things you value most, so you can live your ideal life as quickly and efficiently as possible. There aren't any quick fixes, but whatever phase of life you're in today, I'll help you understand where you stand with your finances and guide you down the path to the quality of life you want. I'll even help you enjoy the journey.

GO ROGUE: Take a few minutes for a self-assessment.

Do you care enough about your quality of life, your freedoms, independence, and security to take the necessary steps so that you maintain or enhance your life$tyle down the road? **Yes / No**

Are you taking the right steps and asking the right questions of your financial team? **Yes / No / I don't know**

What could I be doing to maximize my wealth?

_____

_____

What risks am I taking?

_____

_____

How can I use my wealth to better humanity or creation?

_____

_____

Ladies, these questions aren't just related to your investments. If you're curious about the ways they may apply to your life and wealth, let's talk.

Phone or Zoom.
Schedule your
FREE 15-minute call
with Melissa Myers

https://go.oncehub.com/MelissaMyers

P.S. Don't wait, thinking you'll come back and do it later. Decide now. Go Rogue!

My mom used to ask me, "If everyone jumps off a bridge, are you going to follow them?" Sometimes there is comfort in going along with the crowd. But what I've found, is that there's satisfaction in knowing I've made the right decision for me, even if it's 100% opposite of what everyone else is doing. Let's delve into Chapter 8, "Stop Doing Retirement Like Everyone Else."

YOUR MONEY

Align Your Finances and Values

Stop Doing Retirement Like Everyone Else

If you don't like the road you're walking,
start paving another one.
—Dolly Parton

Already retired? There are nuggets in this chapter for you, too.

If you're nearing the end of your career, are mid-career, or just starting out, this chapter is packed with food for thought and actionable ideas that you can implement to enhance your quality of life.

Retirement is traditionally a much-anticipated, milestone event. However, you don't have to "do" retirement like everyone else. That is, unless you want to! Stay with me because I'm Going Rogue!

You Can Pivot

Regardless of the phase of life you're in right now, you have choices you can make. The financial impact of your decisions will be less painful when you've planned ahead. Planning financially for your future gives you freedoms and options in life and helps prepare you for pivots. You don't have to accept the status quo.

For those of you in the **first half of your working years**, you have license to shake it up. You don't have to play by the same set of rules your parents and grandparents played by. You don't have to be tied down to a specific location. A traditional career might be perfect for you, but if it isn't, no problem. There are ways to make a living and build wealth that don't require you to work in corporate America.

If you're **already retired**, you can choose what to do with your time. Returning to work is an option if you're bored or unfulfilled. Throw the rule book out. You don't have to do the same kind of work you did before you retired. This is an ideal time to expand your horizons and try new things, try doing something you've always wanted to do but never had the time or courage.

Around the age of 50, you may find yourself dreaming of the freedoms you'll have in retirement. You look forward to enriching your life through new experiences and spending time with the people who are important to you. I'd like to propose there may be creative ways to optimize your life sooner, rather than later.

You can retire *whenever* you want as long as you have enough income planned to cover the cost of your life$tyle.

As you approach 60, you'll have lots of decisions to make and details to consider, which is why it pays to hire a CERTIFIED FINANCIAL PLANNER™ to help you figure it all out. Some of the details to consider are:

- Health care costs
- Taxes
- Social Security
- Inflation
- Investment volatility
- Expected and unexpected events
- Income to support your *Lifestyle*

Debt

Paying off debt has the same impact as receiving a raise. Reducing your required outflow each month increases your free cash flow. Less debt means more choices. In retirement, the less you have in debt payments, the less income you need, which means that a smaller retirement nest egg might be okay for your situation. Too much consumer debt is a ball and chain that will keep you working the grind until you're "retirement age" or longer. Living within your means now is great preparation for success at living within your means as a retiree.

Downsize?

Stay with me here. How much equity do you have in your home? If you were to sell your home, what could you do with the equity? Could you use the equity to buy a smaller home or condo? What about renting? Or traveling the country in an RV or boating the Great Loop (remember from Chapter 1)? Less could be more. The popular trends of embracing minimalism and living in tiny houses aren't just for millennials.

Go International

Who says the only place where you can retire is in the United States? Sandy, a single woman in her 50s, has been doing her research. She's looking at countries in Europe and South America. She has a spreadsheet and is analyzing the best places to live based on access to major airports, low crime rates, cultural richness, and health care costs. She's Going Rogue!

Work Forever?

Retirement isn't for everyone. I have clients who say they'll work forever. For them, we aren't planning as much for retirement at a specific age as we are planning for contingencies while they're living their version of their optimal life. These women love what they do and find their work to be highly rewarding. Typically, women in these positions have a great deal of flexibility and are balancing their values, time, and money in a manner that allows them the joy of living their ideal life. You can choose to work indefinitely if you want to do so. Do you love your job enough to do it for as long as you can? I do!

Faith knows she can work for a long time as a realtor. While she has plans in place in case she couldn't work, her profession doesn't "age out" and she can scale back without financial hardship to spend time with her grandbabies.

Other women work so they have something to do. They want structure and purpose and find satisfaction from working.

If you haven't already, it's time to explore your options if you answer "yes" to any of these:

- Are you under so much stress that your health is suffering?

- Are you fed up with your colleagues?

- Are you performing daily mental calculations on the number of days until you can retire?

- Would you like to know what needs to be true of your finances in order to quit today?

Work-Optional

How about having a work-optional life$tyle where you choose when to work rather than being in a financial position of "having to work"?

Suzi left her career as an engineer to be a stay-at-home mom (SAHM). After her first child, she discovered that she missed working and making a financial contribution to the household, so she started a blog, teaching other SAHMs how to build income-generating blogs. Now she works just a few hours a day and has "retired" her husband from his job in corporate America. They sold their home, downsized, and have plans of traveling the country in an RV with their family, while still creating an income. Suzi created a work-flexible life$tyle.

As you get closer to your 60s, with advanced planning, you may want to consider taking a few years off to travel, pick up your art projects, and/or spend time with your family. What's on your bucket list? An extended leave of absence could be the ticket. Especially, if you love what you do and feel like you'd miss it if you weren't doing it anymore.

If you feel the urge to travel or do something else worthwhile, this is the stuff, meaning the type of planning, that people like me love to help you with. I'm not making a blanket recommendation to leave your job for several years in hopes of returning to work, it's just an example of creative ways to maneuver in your 60s.

Location-Flexible

If 2020 taught us anything, it's that we can work from anywhere. And inspiration and motivation can come easily when you live in paradise. Alana has planned for her location-flexible pivot from working in her office to working remotely from

106

a beach town in South America. Technology is her passport to freedom. She's prepared to live anywhere in the world and can do so as long as she has good internet access. Mobile and free from the constraints of a "work until you can retire" mindset, armed with an education, drive, and sense of adventure, Alana has created a way of life that enables her to experience cultural richness and live her happy life abroad.

Your Life Custom-Designed

You've heard the phrase, "Two minds are better than one," so don't be afraid to ask for help. Get a team around you who will understand you and support your goals. It's highly likely that when you ask questions and are open to ideas from your trusted advisors, amazing things can happen.

Your financial team will help you understand whether you're:
- ➲ Utilizing the right types of accounts
- ➲ Leaving money on the table
- ➲ Taking unnecessary risks
- ➲ Prepared for unexpected events

Break Away from Conventional Wisdom

If you want to retire before you're 59½ years old, you need to have an **income plan**. Too many Americans invest solely in tax-deferred retirement accounts, which is what you've been told to do from the time you started working. But, if you want to retire early and don't want a 10% IRS penalty for accessing YOUR money just because you aren't old enough, you have alternative choices.

Retirement accounts were designed to help you save for retirement. However, when it comes to investing for retirement, don't assume the only way to invest is inside of a retirement account.

Also, don't be laser-focused on retirement while neglecting short-term savings and emergency plans. If you're faced with a financial emergency and take an early withdrawal from your retirement accounts, it'll cost you.

Don't let stress rule your life. All you have to do is *ask* for help.

Nontraditional retirement can be your reality. In addition to investment income, you could have income from one or more of the following: Rentals, business(es), income from a "come-back" career, royalties, affiliate income, and part-time work.

BE UNCONVENTIONAL: Rewrite the rules on your retirement.

I love it when clients begin to embrace curiosity about alternative strategies for their finances. A desire for working less and living more is the usual catalyst for asking, "Melissa, what if…?" or "What would it take to…?"

I love these types of questions and am intrigued to understand why she's asking. As long as we can put dollars and dates together, I can help her see the financial impact and opportunities.

It's okay to have a plan that's different from what most people are doing.

Ruth, a seasoned realtor, has been planning and saving her entire career. She has built up a portfolio of rental properties and lives on the rental income, while banking her commissions. When she decides to stop working, her standard of living won't change. She'll still have the rental income that she's been used to living on and will have investments to use for extras.

Your "New" Rules

- ⮑ Start by being curious about alternative strategies to traditional retirement.
- ⮑ Don't buy into retirement myths.
- ⮑ Stop thinking you have limited options.
- ⮑ Remember what brings you joy and find it.
- ⮑ Go ahead and feel the emotions of making your dreams become your reality.

GO ROGUE: What "has" to be doesn't necessarily "have" to be the way you thought.

What's next? Chapter 9, "Stop Ignoring, Procrastinating, and Avoiding." What are you waiting for? Are you waiting because you don't know what to do or how to do it? The sooner you get clarity and advice, the sooner you can live your ideal life!

Stop Ignoring, Procrastinating, and Avoiding

A year from now you may wish you had started today.
—*Karen Lamb*

Now is when we're going to get into the IPA and I'm not talking about beer! Ignoring, Procrastinating, and Avoiding (IPA) are strategies that can hurt you... OR...can they keep you from harm? Let's Go Rogue!

ig·nore
ig'nôr
Disregard intentionally.

pro·cras·ti·nate
prə'krastə,nāt
Delay or postpone action.

a·void
ə'void
Keep away from.

Self-Awareness Check. Do You Speak IPA?

"I'm too busy."

"I can't even deal with that right now."

"I don't want to hear it."

"I don't want to go on a budget."

"I don't want to pay for something that won't benefit me."

"I'm afraid of learning the truth."

"I work hard enough already."

"I don't know how."

"I'll never fix this mess."

"I don't know where to start."

"I'll do that later."

"I'll get to it as soon as I can."

"Let's not go there."

IPAs can be distractions that keep you from getting what you want. On the flip side, IPA strategies can actually help you get what you want. How and when you apply IPA strategies depend on the situation and your desired outcome. Here are some of my personal IPA examples.

I **ignored** the low fuel alert on my gas gauge, which cost me time and money. Because I was running late, I ignored the warning, so that it took me even longer to get to my destination. I had to wait for the tow truck to bring gas so I could go to the station and fill up. I'm glad that I have roadside service coverage as part of my car insurance. Lesson learned. The gas tank is a priority!

I **procrastinated** purging my 13-year-old eye shadow. My skewed thought process was there was still value in the compact, despite common sense telling me I'd gotten my money's worth. Keeping it was just setting me up for the cost and inconvenience of an eye infection from ancient makeup. I'm happy to report that it's in the trash!

I **avoid** the grocery store by having my groceries delivered. Not only do I avoid unhealthy and impulse purchases, I also save time by not driving to and from the store. In fact, as I write this chapter, my shopper is at the store doing the shopping so that we're stocked for the week.

As a result, recently I was able to have Saturday morning coffee, conversation, and much-needed girl time with my friend Liz. I had zero guilt about spending money on a shopping service because I was able to make the most of my time and invest in my relationship with my friend.

It has taken time to get my values and priorities lined up. Now that I have, I use money as a tool to help me live a more meaningful life.

Ignore

Zoe knew where the mailbox was located and that twice a year it would contain her property tax bill. She ignored the mailbox and its contents because the tax bill was such a large amount. Overwhelmed, she ignored the fact that if she didn't pay, she could lose her home. Instead of paying the large tax bill, Zoe paid the minimum on her credit card because she found that bill to be much more manageable.

A budgeting coach helped her gain clarity on her values and priorities. She recognized that her home gave her safety and security and that it was necessary to pay her property taxes to maintain that safety and security. She implemented a system for saving throughout the year, which reduced money stress and made the property tax bills more manageable. Now that she's stopped ignoring the mailbox, foreclosure is no longer her concern!

Conversely, ignoring fear messages put out by the media will *help* you mentally and financially. When you have a sound financial plan, rooted in clarity on your values and goals, you don't need to tune in to mainstream media or the doom-and-gloom headlines that can trigger knee-jerk reactions with your wealth. Think about this: Have you ever noticed that whether the market is up or down, the news anchor uses the same tone? To my ears, they sound negative even when the market closes positive for the day. Ignore fear tactics.

Procrastinate

In the wake of the March 2020 market drop, Roxanne was terrified to find out what it had done to her portfolio. She procrastinated making an appointment out of fear she'd lost her financial security. It took her months to schedule a meeting because she was afraid that all her money had disappeared. Her stress and anxiety were through the roof and stayed high longer than necessary because she delayed learning the truth about her wealth. After the long-dreaded review, she had a pleasant surprise when she discovered that the market, and her portfolio, had rebounded.

Fear of judgment can be the reason you're procrastinating. With me, you're in a judgment-free zone. Early on I made plenty of poor choices, so who am I to judge? I've learned some lessons the hard way and my goal is to help you avoid making the same mistakes that I did **and** to help you to make wise choices going forward.

There is no better time to begin building and protecting your wealth, so procrastinate no longer!

In certain situations, it's *wise* to procrastinate. Procrastination when pressured to make hasty decisions can save you thousands of dollars and keep you from buyer's remorse.

Take for instance the high-pressure timeshare sales tactics at many all-inclusive resorts. In the moment, excitement and high-pressure sales tactics can cause you to agree to the purchase even if, in the back of your mind, you know it isn't the wisest decision. The pressure is there and the pitch is strong because in most cases, a delayed decision results in no sale. More times than not, timeshare purchases cause regret because the decision to say "yes" was made against better judgment.

Not all timeshare purchases incite feelings of remorse. For some, having a timeshare is accountability to follow through on a much-needed vacation. If you look at it from this perspective, go get your rest, relaxation, and rejuvenation!

How have you procrastinated in the past and what have you learned in hindsight?

_____

_____

In what areas of your life are you currently procrastinating? Why?

_____

_____

Arriving at decisions that were difficult to make, are often decisions most worth making.

Avoid

Connie felt like others expected her to make sizable charitable donations and she felt pressure to be the high bidder at fundraiser auctions. Even though her wealth was rapidly dwindling, she continued to give because she didn't want to disappoint, even though it compromised her own financial security.

While she used to give out of a desire to be charitable, it had become a burden now. Connie shared, "Giving at such a high level doesn't feel good anymore." Once she recognized her truth, she avoided fundraisers that weren't her top priority. She also adjusted her level of giving to an amount that made better financial sense for the long term.

Betsy told me she'd been avoiding events where she'd see me and be in a position where she might have to schedule her next appointment. Eventually she booked a meeting and discovered that her finances weren't as bad as she thought. She felt better knowing the truth. With clarity, she realized, "I don't have a lot of room for error, but at least I know where I stand. I have money in savings and investments, a paid-for car, and a zero balance on my credit card. Now I know it is possible to retire in my early 60s."

What could you consciously avoid so that you have a better quality of life?

_____

_____

_____

Are You Ignoring, Procrastinating, or Avoiding Any of These?

- Paying the IRS
- Filing tax returns
- Dealing with debt collectors
- Hiring a financial planner
- Completing your estate plan
- Going to the mailbox
- Paying bills on time
- Earning money

No more ignoring, procrastinating, or avoiding your finances. Liberate yourself. Escape the fear of the unknown by getting guidance—a financial roadmap—for the most efficient route to your desired destination.

115

BE UNCONVENTIONAL: It may seem counterintuitive to spend money on financial advice, however the cost can be well worth the clarity you receive about what you should and shouldn't IPA.

Feel Confident

Know where you stand with your finances and what your options are. Understand when it will serve you to ignore, procrastinate, and avoid certain actions, people, and activities.

Here are a few ways to implement IPAs *for the good*:

⮑ Start avoiding things that are out of alignment with your values and goals.

⮑ Don't let fear of the unknown hold you back from getting guidance.

⮑ Stop wasting your time, money, and energy.

⮑ Do spend your time, money, and energy on that which enriches your life and blesses others.

⮑ Go get answers to your questions.

I urge you to look at life through a new lens and to be conscious of when it is appropriate to ignore, procrastinate, and avoid. If you've been IPA'ing your financial matters and are curious about the process, **here's how I make finances easy and fun!**

1. Conversation
2. Clarity
3. Step-by-step process
4. Actions and accountability
5. Results
6. Monitor
7. Adjust

GO ROGUE: Okay, breaktime. Before moving ahead, grab a snack and glass of water, then go back and journal your responses to the questions in this chapter.

How will you **feel** when you are on YOUR path, living YOUR life? That leads us to Chapter 10, "Do Live Your Life."

YOUR JOY

Experience Peace, Love, and Happiness

CHAPTER 10

Do Live Your Life

*Passion is energy. Feel the power that comes
from focusing on what excites you.*
—*Oprah Winfrey*

I'm Going Rogue! Topics of money, finances, and wealth get set aside in this chapter because my wish for you is that you uncover and embrace that which feeds your soul.

The motivational message, **"Live What You Love,"** resides on the wall in Karmen's office. It's a great reminder to live life to the fullest extent possible. Don't settle. Find your joy in life!

> **BE UNCONVENTIONAL:** All the money in the world won't feed your soul the way that living your life with passion, purpose, and imperfection can.

Purpose

I haven't always known my purpose in life. While I thrived in leadership positions professionally, I was so goal-focused that I felt empty when I'd accomplished all of my goals before turning 40. *Okay, I did it. Now what?*

In pursuit of more, of finding my why, I actively sought out guidance. I was told that I needed bigger goals. That was true, but I also knew I needed more than bigger goals. What I needed was to discover what God intended for me to do while here on earth. In 2015, it came to me while I was at CEO Space International, a business education and networking forum. My purpose is to help others get what they want in life. Simple!

What a relief it was to have this revelation and bask in the simplicity. I was making the job of finding my purpose harder than it needed to be. Confidence in having discovered my why, led to larger goals. Purpose motivates me to push through hurdles and roadblocks. Achieving goals without purpose is a bit of a let-down, so find **your** purpose and experience joy!

121

At the end of the day, I want to know
I added value to someone's life.
—Melissa Myers, CFP®

What I do to serve you is about more than managing investment portfolios, it's about creating an environment and providing structure for a life-changing journey. Beyond finances, there's an opportunity to experience transformation in multiple facets of your life! The value categories we discussed in Chapter 1 are in the forefront of "Do Live Your Life" here:

- ✪ Faith
- ✪ Relationships
- ✪ Health
- ✪ Finances
- ✪ Fun

How Do You Live Your Purpose?

With Passion!

pas-sion
'pa-shən
enthusiasm, excitement, eager interest.

I absolutely love to help solve problems, brainstorm, mastermind, and connect. What do you absolutely love to do? When do you feel excited? In what situations are you eager for more?

I'll propose that your purpose may not be directly related to your career. Also, your motivation in life could have originated from the hard stuff that you've overcome. Get introspective for a moment and consider what you were put here on earth to do.

If you have no idea what your cause is, either because you've never thought about it or you can't figure it out, that's okay. Keep searching and you'll find your answer. It took me nearly 40 years!

Finding your bigger reason and living what you love is a process, not a one-time event. Seek to understand and eventually, you'll understand. Fire up!

With ImPerfection

Allow yourself grace to be imperfect in the midst of your passion. I'm learning to accept that God made me the way I am. **I'm perfect for me**. He made YOU perfect, too. What the world may view as imperfect is just fine in His eyes. We are all works in process and we can all use some daily grace, especially from ourselves.

Even if your actions and the outcomes *aren't* perfect, take a chance to make your life and the world a better place by living your life with passion and intention. My business coaches have encouraged me to get outside of my comfort zone and take imperfect action. What I've learned is that sometimes "good enough" is just perfect!

Focus on the *feeling* you get when you're doing that which fulfills you, and you'll attract those very things into your life.

A New Approach:
- ✓ Start smiling
- ✓ Don't settle
- ✓ Stop getting stuck on why you can't
- ✓ Do focus on what you can do
- ✓ Go forward joyfully

GO ROGUE: Let's get you on the right track and feed your soul by living your life on purpose, with passion, while daring to be imperfect in your quest for peace, love, and happiness.

What do you want to accomplish in life? Revisit Chapter 1 for a refresher or if you've lost sight of what you value and why.

What role does your wealth play in your life's purpose?

_____

_____

Purpose and passion for life is good. So is rest. Slowing down, enjoying people, nature, and beauty fill my soul as do some of the finer things in life. When you have your values and priorities aligned with your money, it's okay to splurge! Chapter 11, "Do Splurge," shares when and how!

Do Splurge

*Three ingredients of luxury lifestyle design
are time, income, and mobility.*
—Tim Ferriss

You can have the freedom to spend money—**to splurge**—on items, activities, and causes that bring you joy. Your money is your tool for living a fulfilled life. Somewhat Rogue!

Remember the lesson Charles Dickens taught us in *A Christmas Carol?* Scrooge was miserable. It wasn't until he started spending money that he experienced joy. You can't take it with you, so you might as well enjoy the results of spending!

As I started coming up with the concept for this book, I thought this chapter was going to be the most fun to write. It seemed like a good idea, because after all, I like nice things as much as you do. Writing about splurges seemed exciting.

splurge
splərj
spend (money) freely or extravagantly.

The conflict I experienced, and I know you've done this too, was my inner dialogue. *What will others think?* The definition of splurge can be taken as a positive or a negative. When I hear that voice, I remind myself that the splurge is my reward, that I've planned for the expense, and it won't derail me from my long-term goals.

What will others think? I'm hopeful and confident that they think, "Well done!" Splurges can be good; something to be anticipated. When you make good decisions, give yourself a reward. The reward is a reminder of what you've **earned and accomplished.**

Then there is the alternate definition of splurge...

ex·trav·a·gant

ik'stravəgənt

lacking restraint in spending money,
costing too much money,
exceeding what is reasonable or appropriate; absurd.

Ouch! Or Ouch?

As I reflected on the description of "extravagant," my initial takeaway was it's bad to be extravagant. I don't want to be bad! So, I decided to "test" each of the definitions of extravagant by asking these questions and encourage you to do the same.

- ➲ Compared to whom?
- ➲ Compared to what?
- ➲ Does it matter?
- ➲ How are "reasonable" and "appropriate" measured?
- ➲ Is that true?

Mindset, Actions, Results

From the time you were born, you were programmed to believe certain things. Your life experiences and environment shaped who you are today, including how you think about money. Your idea of a splurge or extravagance depends on your beliefs and life experiences. You make comparisons to determine what's excessive and what's reasonable and appropriate.

"What others think about you is none of your business," many have quoted. Interesting! I once dated a guy who told me I couldn't afford a certain designer handbag, the one with the famous "LV" logo. He didn't know my financials, so it wasn't an observational statement. He was giving me his unsolicited opinion. In his viewpoint, no one should spend "that much money" on a purse. When I passed the CFP® exam a few years later, guess what I rewarded myself with? Oh yes, I did!

Have you heard these comments before?

"It's ridiculous to spend THAT MUCH money on…"

"Stay out of the living room. You'll ruin the furniture."

"Don't use the good towels."

"You spend *how much* to get your nails done?"

"She'd roll over in her grave if she knew I spent money like I do."

Explaining the guilt about her Vampire Facials, Becky asked, "Who do I think I am? A Kardashian?" The remorse she was experiencing was due, in part, to her concern over what others might think, but it was also because she had no idea how the expense affected her finances in the short or long run.

I want **you** to feel free to splurge. Get the Vampire Facial, but if you experience guilt rather than freedom, I propose that you make time to get clarity on your money and priorities. Having clarity about your values **and** your finances is your ticket to spend freely, to splurge, guilt-free.

Seek Wise Counsel

If you're unsure about how spending today could cost you in the long run, now's the time to start making changes. Invest in yourself and hire professional guidance. When you make improvements in one area of your life, other areas will improve, too. In addition to your financial team, there are various advisors available who guide you on legal matters, taxes, investments, and insurance.

You may also want to seek out additional team members to give you **specialized support** based on their areas of expertise and where you most want to focus and grow.

- ➲ Personal trainer
- ➲ Business coach
- ➲ Career coach
- ➲ Confidence coach
- ➲ Mental health therapist
- ➲ Nutritionist

Initially, it may seem expensive and out of line to hire your team. But remember Chapter 2? The best investment you can make is in yourself. At first, self-improvement may seem like a splurge and more of a want than a need. Over time, because you value yourself and recognize the benefits of life-long personal development, you'll view the cost of your team as one of your top priorities. A necessary expense!

**Confident and empowered women know who they are,
what they stand for, that they can take care of
themselves, and other people's opinions don't matter.**

In Chapter 5, you learned about Sunny Day Funds (SDFs) and how they are more beneficial than a single emergency fund. Designated accounts for specific types of spending help keep you from overspending, while at the same time give you permission to spend! Travel, self-care, giving—whatever is important to you—name the fund and fund it, so that you can splurge!

Ways to Splurge

Upgrade from coach (or fly private!)
Drink champagne (the good stuff!)
Get the designer bags (and shoes)
Take vacations (more than one per year)
Wear your good jewelry (even when you travel)
Enjoy new experiences
Go on excursions
Buy a boat or Jeep or motorcycle
Install a pool in your backyard
Invest in a vacation home
Use the good stuff (towels, pots, silverware, dishes, crystal)
Drive your dream car
Use the valet to park your dream car
Eat lobster
Get a massage (an hour *and* a half)
Refresh with a facial (every month)
Schedule a recurring mani/pedi
Hire a personal trainer
10X your charitable giving
Pick up the tab (for the entire group)
Pay it forward and buy for the person behind you too

Spend freely from your SDFs as long as you have confidence that your decisions won't disrupt you from your long-term goals. If you are unsure, ask for advice. Make your own decisions but get guidance. Understand the consequences of spending and saving. How do your choices today impact your long-term results? Are there any trade-offs?

When you make smart moves with your finances, give yourself rewards.

Do you need some ideas? When you set up systems like SDFs, you'll save time. Reward yourself with an activity you've been holding back on doing.

Think of something you've wanted to do for a long time but have been telling yourself you don't have time to do, or that you can't afford to do. Maybe you leave work early, read a book at the beach, and watch the sunset. Here's another example: Let's say you just paid off the balance of a debt that was costing you $300/month. Consider your values and goals, then allocate part of the $300/month toward your priorities along with a little bump up for your fun money!

"I don't need to take fancy vacations." Is that the truth? Do you think you don't deserve them, that you can't afford to travel, or that vacations are a waste of money? Or are "fancy vacations" just not your thing? However you answer, it's okay. But, if you're feeling like your answer is just a way to rationalize not taking time off for relaxation, let's shift your mindset and plan ahead for your ideal vacation. Sound good?

What I know about myself is that I'm always working. Not out of necessity, but because I love what I do. So, even when I'm not in the office, I'm thinking, planning, learning, and making improvements. I need (and want) vacations, so every month, money is systematically transferred into our "Vacation" SDF. I look forward to seeing new places, checking out of the day-to-day for reading, and relaxing. It's how I rejuvenate. How do you revitalize?

My own journey to financial success took both my **focus** and ability to **balance**. Early on, I concentrated on getting rid of debt, which freed up money for other things.

As my savings and investment accounts grew, I had reserves. Although I could have more reserves today, I value time with my son more than the size of my nest

131

egg. I've spent a lot of money creating memories over the years. The expense was, and is, part of the plan. I have zero regrets. Our annual vacations have been worth every penny, and because it's a planned expense, we can splurge on activities like indoor skydiving!

> **BE UNCONVENTIONAL:** Go for it! Spend money. You've set up and funded your SDFs, so use them!

The Takeaway For YOU?

- ✓ Start having confidence about spending from your SDFs.
- ✓ Don't waste time being wealthy, yet miserable.
- ✓ Stop listening to the opinions of others.
- ✓ Do live empowered—call your own shots.
- ✓ Go joyfully!

Have you ever held back from taking some type of action because you were afraid of what people would think? What splurge would you make right now if you didn't have someone else's voice in your head? Take a few minutes to journal your thoughts.

I've been denying myself _____

For how long? _____

Whose voice is holding me back? _____

What is it saying? _____

Is that actually true? ____ Why? _____

_____

Can I afford to _____?

Will it bring me joy? _____

Now, set your intention for your long-delayed splurge! By what date will you have splurged? _____

The first step I'll take is _____

GO ROGUE: Treat yourself to something luxurious. Splurge!!

The final chapter summarizes how to design and live your ideal life. As you are proactive in taking intentional action steps for your life$tyle goals, remember life is a journey and only you hold the map. Chapter 12 is "Go Rogue!"

YOUR ROGUE!
Play by YOUR Rules

CHAPTER 12

Go Rogue!

Every new beginning comes from some other beginning's end.
—Seneca

Going Rogue! is when you have confidence in your decisions and take actions that are right for you. You're not going to accept the current situation as the only situation. You take a stand for what you believe in and are prepared to go the distance, even opposing the crowd. Own **YOUR Rogue!** and watch what happens!

Goofing off in her backyard with knives (you read that right, KNIVES), Kelly had no idea what was going to happen. You might be thinking, *Playing with knives? Hello, injury! Loss of body parts. Lots of blood. That's what's coming!* I used to think that too. Until I learned more.

Curiosity got the best of me as she told me about the knife throwing league she'd founded. "Throwing knives is empowering, Mel. You should try it. It's really fun; think of it as a competition with yourself." She was right. It IS fun. Lots of other women agree!

Women with Knives (WWK) is a sisterhood that has empowered women of all ages, some of whom were depressed, felt oppressed, lonely, or bored, find happiness, confidence, community, and a passion for life again. Reconnected to their inner strengths that were long forgotten, the women of WWK live life on purpose and with passion. Their bodies and minds are experiencing the thrill of moving after traumatic accidents, they celebrate shedding unwanted pounds, and they own their Rogue! Their idea of fun is playing with knives.

In fact, WWK is now the world's largest women's knife throwing league. Pretty cool bragging rights. Right? While that is impressive, founder Kelly Grove, is nothing but humble. I'm bragging her up because she has been such a blessing to so many amazing women. The opportunity to pick up a knife, aim, and throw it at a target has literally transformed lives!

It's **YOUR** life, play by **YOUR** rules.

How would your life change if you had a new perspective? What if you began looking at situations through a new lens? Who can you bless because you dared to make decisions totally opposite of your previous patterns? Where will your new path take you?

Your Vision, Your Reality!

As you review what I've shared, I want you to feel empowered to take intentional, thought-out steps to live your ideal life. What are you meant to do in your lifetime? While goals are good, purpose is better. Set goals that support your purpose, because without purpose, your accomplishments won't be as fulfilling. With the right mindset, dare to dream big!

As you evaluate your own life areas—Faith, Relationships, Health, Finances, Fun—you'll become more conscious, more aware, of the choices you have and the decisions you make. Your mindset about these life areas is connected to your money behaviors, challenges, and successes. I believe that when you make improvements in one of these areas, you'll see improvements in other areas. I sure have.

Take note of your daily routines and sort out what's truly important to you and your core values. I once had a manager tell me, "If there's something you don't like having to do, stop doing it, and see if anyone notices." You may be surprised that no one is paying attention, so rethink self-imposed, unnecessary scrutiny.

Invest some time and yes, some resources, on yourself. Do activities that replenish your energy and refresh your spirit. Those boosts will result in higher productivity for everything else in your life. Benjamin Franklin said, "An investment in knowledge pays the best interest." I have found that to be very true for my journey. Knowledge opens doors. Taking action gets results; results that are often beyond what you originally imagined.

Live generously. Recognize your skills and expertise can be shared and will likely benefit you as much as others. A simple smile to a harried mom with young children in the grocery store makes a difference. You're acknowledging her, you're valuing her, and it makes a lasting impression for both of you. Be a blessing.

Start with the "end." Where do you ultimately want to be? As you define, refine, and begin the implementation of your purpose-full life, focus on exactly what it is you need to do next and why each step is important to YOU. Don't worry about what others will think.

Remember that your ideal income is the income that is ideal for YOU. Whether you can live on $2,000 a month or feel that $100,000+ a month is ideal, it's up to you. What others think of your income is none of your business—ignore them. You know why you want a certain level of income, so go for it!

Your Financial GPS!

You're reading this book for a reason. I know there's a voice inside of you asking, "What else? Now what? How can I...?"

> *It's the job that's never started that takes the longest to finish.*
> —J.R.R. Tolkien

It's the **getting started** that's the hard part. You're not alone. You can create a team to guide you and hold you accountable. But...Where do you start? Be sure to download your FREE BONUS with this book. It has pages of templates to make your financial journey MUCH easier!

Download your
FREE BONUS
Passport to Freedom Workbook

passport.askmelissamyers.com

An ideal starting point is your *Lifestyle Analysis*. It's the launching point for understanding your financial situation. You'll learn how much money you have coming in, where it goes, and you'll recognize the wealth you've accumulated. When you align your values and goals with your money, you can redirect funds to where you want them to go.

My recommendation is to take small steps and be willing to make adjustments as you implement a new way of managing your finances. I believe that abundance manifests itself when gratitude, love, and kindness play a key role in your day-to-day life. Prepare yourself for the gift of abundance.

Next, keep in mind that money has no power. It is knowledge and action that are powerful. Money is simply a tool to be utilized. For example, by separating your money in an electronic envelope system, you can spend thoughtfully and without guilt. Using my Sunny Day Funds financial approach will open up new freedoms for you. Freedom to go places, savor new experiences, spend time with the people you love, and do the activities you enjoy! Isn't it about time?

We've delved into the layers of mindset and action—past, present, and future—with realistic steps for YOU, taking into consideration a host of variables relative to your situation and where you want to be. Don't assume that money alone is the solution to your level of happiness or financial success; it's the way you think, plan for, and respond to the events in your life that hold the answer.

Your Money!

Much of this book has been a discussion on carefully delineating your "why" and how to align your finances with your values. This adage bears repeating, "Life is a journey and only you hold the map."

The path to your ideal life may take you to some scary places, so get outside your comfort zone and do what you have to do. That way you won't end up attached to your excuses and full of dissatisfaction.

Regarding matters you've been avoiding, empower yourself to pull your head out of the sand because what you don't know can hurt you. And, when you learn the truth, it's usually not as bad as you think it will be. Consider your values in every situation, financial and otherwise, so you can proceed with confidence, tapping into your faith and intuition as your guides for a life free from regrets.

Have you ever performed the necessary car maintenance of tire alignment—after you accidently hit a curb? Likely, you didn't do the actual alignment, you just drove the car to the facility and didn't worry about what the technician would think about you. Same with your finances. You won't have to do the heavy lifting. Just drive yourself to your financial guides who'll do the alignment **without judgment.**

Getting outside your comfort zone can be a big hurdle to overcome. I can relate. Writing books and blog posts, public speaking, and appearing on *Fox News*, *ABC*, and as a guest on multiple podcasts took, and continues to take me, outside of my comfort zone. However, I've realized that I can't let my fear of how others may see me or what they may think distract me from my life's purpose. If I don't accept the challenges, I won't be helping people, and by not embracing these types of opportunities, I'd actually be hurting the women I want to serve.

I feel a sense of great responsibility to serve, not only my clients, but my team, too. If I stay inside my comfort zone and "keep the business simple," I'm not fulfilling my obligations to others. I'd be holding back opportunities for people to get involved, to utilize their talents and expertise.

Instead of trying to do everything myself, I pay others who can do certain jobs faster and better than I can. While I used to view these services as an expense, I now think of them as business efficiencies and a way for others to contribute to my mission of changing women's lives through financial empowerment. Your money mindset and actions can make a positive impact in the world.

Your Joy!

Go for a walk and discover things that give you joy. When it comes to simple pleasures in life, I'll bet they cost little to no money. How do you feel when you see a beautiful sunset, hear the birds singing, or watch a child play? Aren't you grateful for the gift you're receiving at that moment? Be intentional about experiencing peace, love, happiness, and to give yourself grace.

Life is too short to neglect your own needs. If you've been ignoring yours, now is the time to stop. Allow yourself the pleasure of discovering what specifically feeds your heart and soul. Now go do THAT! I advocate rewarding yourself; celebrate your milestones. All of them, not just your financial accomplishments.

My words for the year are: **Give, Live, Serve, Rest**. What are yours? Select key words or phrases that exemplify the direction you've chosen for a given year. Post your words or phrases where you'll see them on a daily basis as a reminder and guide.

The brain is incredible, but scientists share that it can't discern what is truth and what it *perceives* as truth. The more something is repeated, the more the

141

brain believes it to be true. This year, make your truths positive, strong, and reflective of your values. Here are some foundational power words you could incorporate into your financial and life truths:

- ➲ Positivity
- ➲ Maximize
- ➲ Empower
- ➲ Confidence
- ➲ Optimize
- ➲ Freedom
- ➲ Choices
- ➲ Options
- ➲ Impact
- ➲ Legacy

Michele's Story

While finishing this book, I received a very timely note that demonstrates what I've been sharing. But first, a bit of the backstory.

Ever since she worked as a summer camp counselor and swimming instructor, Michele knew she'd found her passion: She was going to become a teacher. You can imagine her feelings of devastation and confusion when, in the final stages of achieving her dream, she was dismissed from her student teaching position due to a personality conflict with her supervisor.

Up to that point, her only focus had been becoming an educator. Understandably, she was scared about what to do with her life. She didn't know how she was going to make a living and get by. But fear didn't stop her. For a few years she worked in a factory, saved up money, and one day, decided to revisit her student teaching experience. It was in 2019, when I was first preparing to write this book, that I received Michele's email, which shared:

> I embraced the challenge. I picked myself back up and got back on my feet. I felt determined and I can say nothing was going to stop me from succeeding. Nothing! I was going to get my teaching certificate no matter what I had to do.

142

I am so glad I had that experience as it made me who I am today. I have valued relationships and have never put money ahead of people. I have always believed if I treat people right, success and money would follow. I can say, lack of money can bring on stress, worrying how the rent will get paid, etc. I didn't want lack of money to control me...I wanted to feel comfortable knowing bills would be paid and that I had a steady place to live. I guess saving makes me feel secure and will give me options in the future. Options to retire from teaching or if I get the chance to teach elementary Phys Ed in the future, I will continue to do that.

Below is an update that she sent me in the spring of 2021:

Hi Melissa, I am excited and happy to let you know I was selected to be the next physical education teacher here at our upper elementary school! Yay! It is official...The principal made the announcement.

Just wanted to let you know the fantastic news. When I was turned down earlier for the lower elementary PE position, I didn't know what to make of it. It was a true character test for me. I didn't know it at the time but there was a reason why it worked out the way it did.

I've been wanting and waiting to teach PE again for 12 years and it is now a reality! I can now teach with the goal of being a blessing and generous to others! I get to follow my heart and passion. Based on my previous experience, the students will love coming to their gym class!

Hope you have a great weekend, and all is well with you! Yay!

Michele accumulated wealth over the course of her teaching career by investing in the retirement plan offered at work and building her own investment portfolio, which included residential real estate rentals. She planned for and created a life$tyle that could be supported without working. My financial planning process helped her see that she was on the right track financially and free to retire in her early 50s.

Proper, prior planning put Michele in the good position of having choices, freedoms, options, and possibilities. While she found it appealing to be able to retire, retirement was trumped by her passion. Having manifested her dream teaching position after 12 years, it was in 2021 that she was offered the Phys Ed position—the position she wrote about in 2019!

Michele no longer needs to work, instead, she is choosing to work because it brings her joy. The beautiful part is her attitude and that she is using the same language I use—about **being a blessing to others and being generous!** I cried happy tears when I read her email because she got what she wanted after years of focus, grit, and maturity.

YOUR Rogue!

What is your version of Rogue? It's your life, so play by YOUR rules. Confident and empowered women filter out the "noise" and focus on what matters, often **blessing others** in the process without even realizing they're doing so. In to-day's world of message overload and agendas, practice the art of discernment. You may discover the messages coming at you don't even apply to you.

In the middle of the 2008 housing crisis that threatened the survival of many American businesses, the Monday morning message from the C-Suite was "Do More! More! MORE!" I knew, deep in my heart, that my team was doing all they could and were doing it very well. We were regularly posting numbers that put us at 130% of our goal. Observing my team's reaction to the messages of "more," I realized they needed to hear a different message and I had a decision to make. They needed to hear my message. I chose to **GO ROGUE!** "They aren't talking to us. Keep doing what you're doing!"

In your life, both professionally and personally, you've got choices to make, and choices are fun! You get to choose where to live, when to retire, and how to spend your time. Even if you're already retired, you still have choices that can take you abroad, to a larger home, smaller home, and maybe even multiple homes. You can live in a home on wheels or a home that floats. Even in a home with goats, perhaps serving a nonprofit or church ministry.

Consider your choices and listen to your instincts about the areas of your life that need attention. Seek honest feedback from wise counsel. How would you benefit from self-development? Personal growth prepares you for the future. From **relationships** to your **health**, your money can be a tool to mend, en-hance, and serve. What are some positive outcomes you've experienced because you invested in yourself?

Own YOUR Rogue!

In good times and bad, remember to focus on what you can control. When was the last time you thought about the following?

What's Within My Control

generosity

my thoughts

what I read

kindness

my attitude

questions I ask

my actions

my nutrition

how I spend time

my subscriptions

how I spend my $

how I vote

what I watch

my appearance

what I listen to

physical exercise

Going Forward

It has been said that, "Procrastination is the enemy of wealth." Now is the time to embrace that it is **your** life—you can play by your rules. Rules that aren't arbitrary, meant for the general public, or in our context of financial planning, even those meant for a typical investor. Instead, you can take custom-designed action steps to gain financial success that makes sense for you and your situation.

> **BE UNCONVENTIONAL:** We know that personal finance is personal, which involves part heart, part head. It's quantitative and qualitative. Your life, your wealth, your rules. It's your ideal, not anyone else's.

Live YOUR Life by Design

You can have everything you want in life. It just comes at a price. You pay with time and/or money. I encourage you to get creative with your dreams, goals, and purpose. Money shouldn't be your excuse. Decide what's important to you and commit to doing whatever it takes to make it happen.

Get in the right frame of mind. Surround yourself with like-minded, positive people. Maintain your focus. You can default into your life, finances, and retirement, or you can live life by your design. It's never too late. And…The earlier you plan, the **more choices** you'll have.

WHAT'S NEXT?

Many financial professionals will say they can help anybody. I used to say that, too. When I first started investing in myself, even after paying thousands of dollars for business coaching, I was afraid to take my coach's advice. She challenged me to create marketing messages that would attract my ideal client.

I knew who I enjoyed working with and what "ideal" meant to me, but I was terrified that I'd alienate and offend my existing clients. I didn't want to lose them. After getting outside my comfort zone and changing my approach to speak directly and more to the needs and wants of my target market; my clients, including men, have stayed with me and by narrowing my scope, I've been able to serve even more women on their wealth journey!

Who do I work with? Typically, I work one-to-one with women who are single or are the financial decision maker in their household. Usually, she's at a high point in her career where she's making more money than she ever has and wants to make sure she isn't making mistakes or leaving money on the table.

She wants to feel secure, to have her freedoms, and independence. She doesn't want to be a burden to others. Often, it's a recent experience, some kind of life event that triggers her to reach out to me: A death, divorce, career changes, an inheritance, or settlement. She is busy and doesn't want the entire financial responsibility to be on her shoulders. She wants to pass the torch to a team who'll guide her, so she can spend time doing the things she enjoys doing and being with the people she loves. Do you know anyone who might be curious?

I know there are many women, women like you, who want and need my help. There's a limit to the number of clients I can serve in a one-to-one format. That's why I've created multiple ways to serve you. In addition to financial planning, investing, and insurance, I provide **Life$tyle Coaching**, courses, and workshops. I write for those of you looking for more information. Also, I've committed to developing my skills as a public speaker so I can inspire and motivate groups of women into action for better outcomes with their finances.

You are a smart woman. You succeed in life and in your calling. But you don't have to be all things to everybody, and you certainly don't have to do it all on your own when it comes to your finances. Just *ask*.

If what I write, speak, and teach resonates with you, if you're ready to pass the torch from going it alone with your finances and ready to take action to relieve the burden, do it now. Take a moment to book your appointment with me.

Phone or Zoom.
Schedule your
FREE 15-minute call
with Melissa Myers

https://go.oncehub.com/MelissaMyers

147

YOUR ROGUE!

The sooner you take action, the sooner you'll feel better and be able to amplify and live your ideal life while blessing others!

Yesterday ended last night. Today is a brand-new day.
—Zig Ziglar

Start with discernment.

Don't listen to the noise.

Stop fueling chaos.

Do less, accomplish more.

GO ROGUE!

Acknowledgments

To my clients and the more than 100 women I interviewed, this book is yours! Even if you aren't specifically named, there is a piece of you in this book. I believe that you, every single one of you, has a unique and powerful story that can make a positive impact on this world. I hope you Go Rogue!

I'd like to thank my book launch team for your friendship, support, promotion, and imbedded accountability to get this book out to the world.

Tony Rubleski and Paul Guyon, your coaching was the spark that led me to implement. First it was writing blogs, then *Journeys to Success Volume 9*, and now *Going Rogue!*

Sweet Potato Fries, I was scared when I shared my first piece of writing with you. Thanks for welcoming me and helping me develop my confidence, voice, and writing skills. Janet Vormittag, Lee Bradley, Donna Hinman, Susan Maciak, and Wendy Coon, I appreciate you and value your expertise.

Karlyn DeGram, Hannah Zeigler, and Yulia Pervushina, you created a winning cover!

Julie LeMieux and Taryn Schnoebelen, thank you for being team players and allowing me to stay focused.

For edits and feedback, Kelsey Turek, Rachel Williams, Rachelle Osborn, Tammy Stone, Tracy Bailey, Carly Niemier, Emilee Duell, Tonya Christiansen, and Ben Hudelson. Sarah Kallio, thank you for your edits AND the illustrations!

To my mentor and coach, Robyn Crane, thank you for encouraging me to get outside my comfort zone and conduct book interviews. Look what happened!

My wish is that this book is a blessing to women worldwide. Thanks to The BE Event and The Hope Project for your strategic partnerships.

Mom and Dad, I am the woman I am because of you. Sisters, Holly Larsen and Rebecca Kelley, thank you for supporting me along this journey.

ACKNOWLEDGMENTS

To my husband, Ryan Myers, and son, Brock Brieger, you gave me space and encouragement to write. Both of you picked up the slack around the house. Thank you for helping me "work on my book."

Without the Epic Author Publishing team, this book would still be an idea in my mind and a goal on my bucket list. Trevor Crane, thank you for creating, designing, and refining your incredible resources, including your team: Ashley Peterson, Jess and Jo Todtfeld, Julie DeLucca-Collins, Dr. Travis Parry, and my rock, Ann Niemann.

It took me a while and eventually I figured it out. Goals are good. *Your* purpose is better. Thank you, God, for your faithfulness, love, and grace.

My Story: Journey To Success

You Can Do Whatever It Is You Set Your Mind To

By Melissa Myers, CFP®

[First published by Melissa Myers as Chapter 4 in *The Tom Cunningham Tribute: Journeys to Success*. Based on the success principles of Napoleon Hill. Copyright ©2018 by John Westley Publishing ISBN 978-1-947560-05-5.]

It's a sunny, spring day in 2018. The kind of day where the sun has warmed the room enough to warrant opening the windows and doors allowing cool, fresh air inside. I sit in the sun watching the ducks play in the water. A pair of bald eagles are perched in a tree in front of me. Laughing to myself, I think, *Who needs a TV? Mother Nature is the ultimate entertainment center.*

Spring Lake, Michigan has provided me with entertainment and inspiration over the years. I've had a lot of fun in the sun, boating with friends on the very lake I'm now lucky enough to live on. Twenty years ago, if you and I were boating on Spring Lake and you told me, "One day you're going to live up there, on that hill, in your brand-new house, with an inground pool, and you'll have paid cash for your last four vehicles," I wouldn't have believed you.

Over the last couple of decades, I've kept in mind my mom's encouraging words: "You can do whatever it is you set your mind to." While I can't remember the events or circumstances of my childhood and teen years that led to conversations when my mom spoke these encouraging words, I've adopted and applied the belief, time and time again.

Perhaps my mom read *Think and Grow Rich* and was giving me her interpretation of what Napoleon Hill wrote and taught.

Whatever your mind can conceive and believe, your mind can achieve.
—Napoleon Hill

In first grade I took gymnastics. I loved the challenge, and I wasn't scared. There was one stunt that I really wanted to be able to do: The Penny Drop. I hung by my knees on the lower bar of the uneven parallel bars. I swung back and forth as I tried to get enough momentum so that I would be able to release my knees and land on my feet.

155

Time after time, I fell. At some point, the coach looked at me and said, "You might want to stop that so you don't get hurt." I wasn't dissuaded. Rather, I was determined. I knew I could do it; I just needed to keep trying. That very night, after many falls, I finally nailed the stunt. In my mind, I knew I could do a Penny Drop. I kept trying until I finally succeeded.

In high school, Mr. Pattison taught the typing class. He would have us cover our hands with a sheet of paper so we couldn't see our keyboards and dictate the keys we were to type: "f, d, s, a, space, j, k, l, semicolon."

Driven to perfection, each night as part of my winding down process, I'd lie in bed and "type": "I-h-a-v-e-a-b-i-o-l-o-g-y-t-e-s-t-t-o-m-o-r-r-o-w." I don't know how I ever thought to visualize myself typing each letter of every word in my head. What I do know is that the visualization exercise was highly effective; my speed and accuracy improved significantly by the end of the year.

After nearly ten years of snow skiing, I got serious and took lessons. The instructor taught me to visualize the path my skis would take based on the instructions I gave my body. Use your feet to turn your skis. Your outside ski is the ski you put pressure on to turn. When you want to turn left, put your weight on your right ski. When you want to turn right, shift your weight from your right foot to your left foot.

You can ski any run if you stay in control. When you're on the chairlift, envision yourself making perfect turns, starting at the top and all the way down the entire hill. On the chairlift, in the car, and before I fell asleep each night, I would execute perfect runs in my mind. By the end of the season, my turns were fluid, and I was confident on the black diamonds.

In my 30s, my Big Hairy Audacious Goal (BHAG) was to pay off my mortgage before I turned 40. I believed I could and I did! How did I accomplish such a big goal?

Early on, I had gone into debt. Going into debt was easy. When I bought my first car, I got a loan. When I turned 18, I applied for a credit card—many credit cards. College? Student loans. Clothes? Credit cards. Car maintenance? Credit cards. Vacations and restaurants? Credit cards.

When I was 26 and about to move for a new job, I received advice from many well-intentioned people. Buy a house. Making mortgage payments is better than paying rent. You're building equity.

A short time after I bought my first home, I was hired at Morgan Stanley Dean Witter as a Financial Advisor. Two years later, I was struggling to hit my numbers. I didn't have marketing expertise or referral sources to help me bring in new clients and be successful. Each month, I was going deeper and deeper into debt. Amassing debt is easy. Getting out of debt is a challenge.

Eventually, I started to feel the stress of having too many bills and not enough income. The other thing I started to struggle with was shame and embarrassment. I'd been a financial advisor for two years, yet I was the one who needed advice. While I taught my clients how to invest and how to protect themselves with various forms of insurance, I was unable to help them with basic money management. I decided to quit my job as a financial advisor. Not long after I quit, I took a position as a licensed sales assistant in another Morgan Stanley office.

Budget Your Time and Money

Even though I went from commission-based to salary when I took the sales assistant position, I continued to go deeper into debt. Scared into desperation and humbled, in September 2003 I allowed my sister, Becky, to help me make a budget. She also lovingly told me to quit the gym, stop tanning, and stop getting my nails done. She gave me Dave Ramsey's book, *Financial Peace*, and I learned about Dave's famous "debt snowball."

I began to budget my time and money. I began to act with intention. Exercising Personal Initiative (from the Ramsey book), I humbled myself and followed my sister's advice. First a student, later a teacher, I planned ahead for expenses and created a get-out-of-debt plan. I began saying, "no" to things that cost money and weren't adding value to my life. People thought I was cheap. Others wondered why I wrote checks to myself. Those checks were my "allowance" or spending money for the week. I budgeted my money over time.

Track. Project. Adjust. Repeat. It became apparent that I needed more income. I decided to become a Pampered Chef© consultant. After all, I loved to cook. I thought, if I could cook and earn money while helping others get the right tools in their kitchens, it was a bonus. Also, by working some extra nights and weekends, I wouldn't spend money I didn't have.

157

The decision to become a Pampered Chef consultant was one of the best decisions I ever made. Why? A guest at one of the parties decided to become a consultant. While I was training her, she recognized something in me that I didn't see in myself. She knew I'd been a financial advisor, was currently a licensed assistant, and that Pampered Chef was my side-hustle. She said, "You need to be **advising**, not assisting. Give me your resume."

She worked at a bank and passed my resume to a co-worker. The co-worker passed my resume on to his competitor at another bank, and I got the job as a Financial Advisor/Associate Team Leader!

The week I started my new job, we had a corporate sales conference. At dinner one night, one of my peers told me, "You just got the opportunity of a lifetime. This job can be life changing…If you do it right." I'll never forget those words.

After about nine months into my new position and its learning curve, I still was struggling to meet my sales goals. I began to question whether I should even be a Financial Advisor.

One morning, while getting ready for work, I prayed, "God, if you want me to be a Financial Advisor, please put the people in front of me that you want me to help."

By Applied Faith

Within a month, two very significant things happened. One, at the next sales conference, we were told to set a goal of selling $35,000 in investments per day. If we did that, we'd hit our goal. Okay, great! And thank you! Now I had a numeric goal to pursue.

The second thing that happened was that my manager asked me if I would like to cover some other offices. This was THE opportunity I'd been waiting for. I was so excited. Armed with a numeric sales goal and the chance to work in offices that had the potential to produce higher numbers, I began to meet success, personally and professionally.

At that time, we were paid quarterly, based on the sales we had written. The last week of the quarter came with a big "push" from corporate to sell as much as possible. Driven to hit my sales goals, I pushed myself. Up to that point, I lived on a budget and paid a little bit each month toward my debt, but it was taking a long time. The end-of-quarter-push paid off. The incentive was large enough so that I was able to pay off $10,000 worth of debt! My quarterly incentive check was truly life changing.

The taste of financial reward fueled my drive and further motivated me. It also gave me confidence that I could earn enough to dig myself out of a deep hole of debt. Every incentive check went toward debt. Credit cards, student loans, and a loan from my mother-in-law were paid off. After that, it was my car loan. A short time later, my boss told me he was taking a position elsewhere and that I should let our regional manager know that I was interested in the Team Leader position.

The next day, the regional manager and I met. He didn't make any promises. Even without a promise, I acted in good faith that the job would be mine.

The Extra Mile

For three months, I fulfilled responsibilities of the role and acted as if I already had the promotion. I believed if I demonstrated my capabilities and went above and beyond what was expected of me, I would get the promotion. What surprised me was my quarterly incentive check. While I hadn't been given the title, I received the compensation. Management paid me as if I were the Team Leader. Shortly after I received the largest check of my life, I received the official promotion!

Definiteness of Purpose

In a position where I was able to help clients and train others how to help clients, I found fulfillment and confirmation. I fully knew that I was doing what I was meant to do. God put opportunities in front of me, and I embraced them. I'd found my chance to live my life with definiteness of purpose.

I learned from my personal struggles with money and used that experience to help friends, clients, and colleagues make changes and improve their financial situations. While money is important, I understood that people mattered more than money. I approached others with a servant mentality: "How can I help you?" and "What are you working on?" and "What are your goals?"

Establish a Mastermind Alliance

It takes a team to build success. During the 2008 housing crisis, Monday morning meetings were a time to brainstorm and collaborate, a time to share best practices. We knew that three minds were better than two, and without knowing what a mastermind alliance was, we acted as one. Simply put, we defined a goal, designed a collaborative plan to achieve it, and held ourselves accountable. Rather than complain about change or challenges, we would ask questions. How can we get this done? What do we need to learn? What do we need to do? There's got to be a better way.

One idea led to another. We learned from each other. We trusted one another. We held each other to a higher standard. Achieving 100% wasn't good enough. We decided to set our goal at 130%, and we surpassed that, too. We maintained a **positive mental attitude** about success.

I've continued to seek out different groups of individuals to work collectively as a mastermind alliance, tailored to the task in executing new goals for professional or volunteer projects.

Budget Your Time and Money

Having budgeted my time and money, paid off. I **went the extra mile** and studied for industry exams that weren't required of me. I earned licenses and the CERTIFIED FINANCIAL PLANNER™ designation. The more I studied, the less time I had to watch TV or spend money. The investment I made in myself led to more opportunities.

Over the course of six years and a divorce, I paid off all my debt including my mortgage, while still being able to travel and have an inground pool installed. Most people will tell you that a pool is a waste of money. If you don't use it, I'd agree. However, some of my best memories are of time spent with friends and family in that pool. I feel I got every dollar's worth and more!

Cultivate Creative Vision

In 2010, I started to date Ryan. He liked to go out on his boat, and I liked to go into my backyard and enjoy the pool. While dating I wondered how we could have both a pool and a boat without all the hassle of packing, loading, unloading, and unpacking with every excursion. There might be a better way. Poolside one evening, I suggested, "If we had a house on the water with a pool, I'd go for a boat ride with you whenever you wanted." We started to look at waterfront homes for sale on Zillow.

Property values were still quite low due to the "Great Recession." We crunched some numbers and were ready for a new challenge. We decided we could buy a waterfront home. We just wouldn't live in it right away. For five summers, we would rent out the lake house as a weekly vacation rental. After five years, we would sell the house we lived in, use the proceeds to pay off the vacation rental, remodel it, and move to the water.

We made an offer on a lakefront home in September 2011. We closed on our waterfront home, and I sat for the CFP® exam in November. We got married in December.

I accomplished my goal of paying off the mortgage before I turned 40. I found out that I'd passed the CFP® exam in the spring of 2012. Life was going according to plan.

It was around that time that I started to get bored with my job. I began to feel a disconnect between how I wanted to serve my clients and the culture in which I worked. You need to have at least four sales appointments a day. What are you doing to make sure you hit your numbers? Melissa, what's going on with your offices? We're going to introduce your new comp plan for the upcoming year. It only has a few changes.

I began to feel a strange sense of anxiety. The interesting thing is that I wasn't anxious or overwhelmed with tasks and projects. Up to this point, most of my free hours were spent studying, designing a backyard, building out an unfinished basement, planning a wedding, and starting a vacation rental business.

I was anxious because I had nothing new and creative to do. I'd accomplished all my goals; I hadn't made any new goals, and I began to drift.

Learn from Adversity and Defeat

I didn't drift for long. Shortly after I received the letter congratulating me on having passed the CERTIFIED FINANCIAL PLANNER™ exam, I had a new goal. I applied for a regional manager position, which would entail managing Team

Leaders. Armed with experience in leadership, I was ready for a new challenge and opportunity. I was confident in my ability to lead. Decision makers had other ideas as to where I would be most useful. Why take a successful producer out of production? I didn't get the management position.

In August 2012, I decided to leave corporate America and start an independent financial planning practice with my friend and colleague, Karmen Gearhart. Over the years we had disciplined ourselves to **budget our time and money**. That put us in the financial position to build our business from the ground up without incurring any debt. Years later, I have no regrets. I'm grateful that I didn't get that regional management position because it prompted me to set an even bigger goal.

Combine Personal Initiative with Definiteness of Purpose

It takes a lot of **personal initiative** to start and run a successful business. When faced with the challenges of running a business, I remind myself that I'm serving others as they seek to improve their position in life. It's my **definiteness of purpose**. It's what drives me to stay focused. I love to see others overcome adversity and achieve their goals and dreams.

In the financial world you can find success by doing high volume or you can be strategic with fewer, yet bigger clients. At the bank, we had a large team, and we did high volume. As an independent advisor, we had neither the volume nor large team. Logic told me, "It's time to find your niche."

I ran client demographic reports and started to identify a few trends. However, the data didn't clearly suggest that I had any specific niche.

Actions Prove the Practicality of Our Imaginations

A few months into opening my financial planning practice, I partnered with Wendy Coon to give "Health and Wealth" presentations. Wendy asked Tony Rubleski to coach us. Soon after, Tony and Paul Guyon invited me to join their Mastermind group. I was introduced to the books *Think and Grow Rich, The 4-Hour Workweek*, and the business networking group CEO Space International.

CEO Space International helped me get clarity about two challenges.

One, while I wanted to "niche down" to fewer, bigger, better clients, I had a burning desire to help people who were without significant wealth. My heart was telling me to serve those who had financial challenges and were ready to take the steps toward improving their financial situation. My challenge was how to serve both a niche with wealth and people without wealth.

Imagination

CEO Space International staff helped me see that I could serve both groups at the same time. Many of the staff had clients with whom they worked on an individual basis. They also had multiple income streams from sources that included physical books, e-books, courses they created, and group coaching. They put on exclusive events, created membership groups and websites, wrote blogs, and did public speaking.

How did they do all of that? They created products they could sell, and they built scalable businesses. Aha! I could do that too! I could serve both my niche clientele along with the mass market by creating a scalable business model.

Secondly, I found clarity on my desire and ability to "give back" financially. One afternoon, the founder, Berny Dohrmann, gave us the opportunity to make a public announcement. He asked us to stand up and share what it was that we committed to implement once we got back home. Having carried student loan debt into my 30s, I decided to start a scholarship fund. My objective was to help reduce or eliminate the need for recipients to have student loan debt.

Back home, three months later, I met with Holly Johnson from the Grand Haven Area Community Foundation, and on July 8, 2015, I signed the agreement where I committed to making monthly contributions to start a scholarship fund.

Enthusiasm and Concentration

The same summer that I started the scholarship fund, I read _The 4-Hour Workweek_. Next, I searched for blogs and podcasts on passive income. Pat Flynn's _Smart Passive Income_ came up in Google. Each morning, I listened to his podcasts while I got ready for the day. I learned about passive income from affiliate marketing. Then an idea popped into my head: I would create a blog and the money I made from affiliate sales would help me get the scholarship fund fully funded ahead of schedule.

Thanks to Suzi Whitford at "Start a Mom Blog," I learned how to build websites, write blog posts, and make images for Facebook, Pinterest, Instagram, and my blog posts. Through online courses, podcasts, and webinars I recognized a framework existed where I could create and deliver information online with courses, books, podcasts, blogs, classes, and video.

More Applied Faith

"OK, but how do I put it all together?" I knew it could be done. I just didn't know how. My question was answered by my coach, Robyn Crane. Robyn taught me how to build programs and packages so that I can serve my clients at a higher level.

Had I not been willing to try new things, meet new people, or engage in generosity of time, money, and expertise, I wouldn't be serving the clients that I am today. Nor would I be able to serve the people whom I'll be serving in the future. Due to my personal initiative, I've accomplished more than I ever thought possible. Because of applied faith, I know this is just the beginning and more great things are yet to come. As I achieve goals, I'll set bigger goals centered around my definiteness of purpose: Helping people!

> *Whatever your mind can conceive and believe,*
> *your mind can achieve.*
> —*Napoleon Hill*

A component of our original, five-year vacation rental plan was that we would do a major remodel of the lake house before we moved into it. The timeline changed when we sold the house we lived in, two years earlier than planned. We lived in the lake house for three years and didn't do any improvements because we knew we'd remodel soon. I wanted to remodel and use as much of the existing structure as possible to keep what we could out of a landfill.

Many people told us we'd be better off if we did a complete demo and started from scratch. In my naivety, I didn't believe them. Confident that a remodel was the way to go, we had our pool installed.

After nearly two years of research, planning, pinning to my Pinterest boards, and ongoing meetings with an architect, we were ready for bids from builders. The people who told us to tear down and start over were right. The bids came in excessively higher than planned and beyond what we wanted to spend, especially on a remodel. I was crushed, not to mention, mentally exhausted. I'd spent hours and hours of my time researching and planning the remodel.

However, I'm not a quitter. I went back to the drawing board, literally. A year later, we moved into our brand-new home. It cost substantially less than the remodel estimates, much closer to our original budget, and is laid out and designed to our taste and lifestyle. The pool is done, the boat will be coming out of storage soon, and we're ready to enjoy summer in West Michigan!

Build A Positive Mental Attitude

Despite challenges, setbacks, and adversity, I've been able to create plans and implement them to achieve goals. I remember my mom's words of encouragement and focus on getting an answer to my question, "How am I going to...?" Today, I'm humbled and grateful. I've learned from my challenges, and I use those experiences to serve others as they seek to improve their position in life—**My definite purpose!**

TRIBUTE TO TOM

"You can do it." Tom, I am grateful for you, your beliefs, and the work you did to make the world a better place. Although we never met in person, your emails, and words of encouragement, "You can do it," motivate and inspire me to do work that makes this world a better place. Thank you for allowing me to contribute to Volume 9 of *Journeys to Success*. Warmly, Melissa Myers, CFP®

Kar-Mel
FINANCIAL PLANNERS

Take all this knowldege
to the next level with 1 to 1
financial planning, investment
and insurance solutions so
that you can have the time
and financial freedom you desire.

READY?

Phone or Zoom. Schedule a FREE 15-minute call:
https://go.oncehub.com/MelissaMyers

About the Author

Melissa Myers, CFP® lives in Spring Lake, Michigan with her husband, Ryan, and son, Brock. She is a member of the Lake Michigan Estate Planning Council, Counterpart, the Grand Haven Eagles, Tri-Cities Women Who Care, and Toastmasters.

Giving back to the community is important to Melissa. In support of the local arts, she served a seven-year term as a board member for the West Michigan Symphony Orchestra and has established a scholarship fund with the Grand Haven Area Community Foundation. A woman of faith, she's a member of All Shores Wesleyan Church, where she volunteers in the personal finance ministry.

Melissa loves to travel and is a self-proclaimed foodie in search of fabulous restaurants specializing in unique and amazing food (ask for recommendations!). At home, she loves cooking, boating, and relaxing poolside with a great book. She stays active by skiing, playing tennis, and going to spin class.

ABOUT THE AUTHOR

Professionally, Melissa has over two decades' experience empowering women with their finances. She earned the prestigious CERTIFIED FINANCIAL PLAN-NER™ designation in 2012 and became a certified Faith and Finances facilitator in 2016.

Regardless of where someone might be on the wealth spectrum, she believes everyone can benefit from a financial road map, as her clients attest. Testimonials share they view Melissa as their financial GPS in helping determine where they are, where they want to be, and in providing the services to pursue their financial destination.

In addition to running her own financial planning practice and serving her clients, Melissa is a speaker, author, leader, and has been a guest on ABC and Fox News along with multiple podcasts. She wrote Chapter 4 in *Journeys to Success, Volume 9*, sharing how she applies the success principals of Napoleon Hill in her life.

Connect with Melissa:

Websites: www.askmelissamyers.com

              www.karmelfp.com

Facebook: www.facebook.com/melissamyers.karmelfinancialplanners

LinkedIn: www.tinyurl.com/LinkedinMelissaMyers

Melissa Myers, CFP®

Your wealth journey is my passion and I'm on a mission to help women like you. I believe that when your money and values are in alignment, you can live an optimized life full of satisfaction and blessings.

I know your situation is unique; therefore, your strategies should be too. Prior to opening Kar-Mel Financial Planners, I was a manager and financial advisor at The Huntington Investment Company and a financial advisor at Morgan Stanley.

Over the years, I came to understand that my clients desired personalized advice and custom strategies to address their financial questions, frustrations, and concerns. In 2012, it was time to deliver. Kar-Mel Financial Planners was born!

If you would like to receive your financial advice in a boutique atmosphere rather than a "big box" firm, let's talk.

Made in the USA
Columbia, SC
19 March 2022

57599054R00104